LITTLE BOOK OF BIG IDEAS

Philosophy

First published in the United States of America in 2007
by Chicago Review Press, Incorporated
814 North Franklin Street
Chicago, Illinois 60610

Conceived and produced by
Elwin Street Limited
144 Liverpool Road
London N1 1LA

Illustrations: Richard Burgess, Emma Farrarons
Designer: Thomas Keenes

ISBN-13: 978-1-55652-663-3
ISBN-10: 1-55652-663-6

Printed in China

LITTLE BOOK OF BIG IDEAS

Philosophy

Dr. Jeremy Stangroom

CHICAGO
REVIEW
PRESS

Contents

Introduction

Philosophy ... sees the familiar as if it were strange, and
the strange as if it were familiar. It can take things up
and lay them down again. Its mind is full of air that
plays round every subject. It rouses us from our native
dogmatic slumber and breaks up our caked prejudices ...

William James, *Some Problems of Philosophy*

According to philosopher Wilfred Sellars, "The aim of philosophy
is to understand how things in the broadest possible sense of the
term hang together in the broadest possible sense of the term." It
is with this thought in mind that this book has been put together.
It features fifty of the world's greatest thinkers; not all are
philosophers in the strict sense of the word — Max Weber is a
sociologist, for example, and Lawrence Kohlberg, a psychologist
— but all of them have things to say which are of philosophical
interest. In addition, the book looks at ten broader concepts and
movements, each of which has played a part in the history of
philosophy and the social sciences. The hope is that, taken
together, these two aspects will give readers a good flavor of
the sorts of issues that people think and talk about in the name of
philosophy.

It is a truism that there is something arbitrary about the
selection of thinkers included in a book such as this. No doubt
there will be complaints that philosopher X, a veritable genius, is
absent, whereas Y, a mediocrity at best, is present. A quizzical
look suffices as a response to such complaints. There is no
suggestion here that this book comprises a definitive top fifty of
the world's greatest thinkers. Such a thing is not possible.

The thinkers included here are among the finest the world has known. But there are, of course, many others just as fine.

This is a short book; philosophers write long books, and frequently many of them. Therefore, it has been necessary to make some compromises when talking about their ideas. The strategy that has been adopted here is to take one or two of the major arguments of each philosopher, and to look at these in a little bit of detail. The idea is to give the reader a sense of what it is like to make a philosophical argument; the kinds of moves and counter-moves that are involved in such an endeavor.

Some people — and unfortunately more than a few professional philosophers — will sneer at the notion that it is possible to deal with philosophy in a book such as this. Ignore the sneers. It is true, of course, that if you want to be a professional philosopher, then you've got to know the detail of established philosophical arguments (though Wittgenstein apparently did not). But you don't have to know these details to get a sense of what philosophy is about and an insight into the ideas which engage philosophical minds. So read this book; if you then decide that you want to be a philosopher, it will be time to read what the great philosophers have to say in their own words.

Arguably, what defines philosophy is a particular way of thinking. It requires the ability to follow logical argument; to play with different ideas to see where they lead; to anticipate objections and counter-arguments; to be willing to put aside preconceptions in the interests of a detached objectivity. In this sense, philosophy is not so much the love of wisdom, as the Ancient Greeks would have had it, but rather the love of argument, and the hope that good arguments will lead to wisdom. If this book succeeds in introducing its readers to some of the best arguments ever made, then it will have done its job.

Dr. Jeremy Stangroom

Introduction

Pythagoras

According to Bertrand Russell, Pythagoras was one of the most important philosophers that ever lived. To a modern mind, this might seem a little odd, especially when one considers that Pythagoras founded a mystical religion, which was based on a belief in immortality and metempsychosis, and which included amongst its rules that one must abstain from eating beans, not touch a rooster, and not let swallows share one's roof. However, there was another side to Pythagoras: a contemplative, rational side, which enabled him to make some of the earliest advances in mathematics.

Born: Ca. 580 BC, Samos, Ionia, Greece
Importance: Showed how reality could be understood in terms of numbers
Died: Ca. 500 BC, Metapontum, Lucania, Magna Graecia (now Italy)

It is, of course, well known that the theorem which makes it possible to calculate the length of the hypotenuse of a right-angled triangle from the length of its sides is credited to Pythagoras. However, this is only a small part of the legacy that he bequeathed to mathematics. Perhaps more significantly, he is thought to have discovered the mathematical foundations of music. It is said that he first came to a realization of the relationship between mathematics and music whilst watching blacksmiths at work. He noted that the pitch of the sounds produced as a hammer struck an anvil varied according to the weight of the hammer. This insight was developed by his followers, who

> As long as man continues to be the ruthless destroyer of lower living beings he will never know health or peace. For as long as men massacre animals, they will kill each other.
>
> Pythagoras

realized that the lengths of the strings of a lyre required to produce the notes of a scale could be determined in terms of precise mathematical ratios. Thus, the beauty of music was shown to be underpinned by a mathematical structure.

For Pythagoras and his followers, this was a clue to the ultimate structure of reality; they believed that behind the realm of appearances "all things are number." It isn't, however, quite clear what they intended this to mean. The problem here is that no writings by Pythagoras himself survive; all that we have to go on are fragments of his teachings, seemingly written by his followers. Nevertheless, Russell suggests that it is likely that Pythagoras was committed to a molecular view of reality; that he thought that bodies were ultimately composed of individual atoms. This would render them susceptible to mathematical analysis, thus fitting with his view that all things are number.

The influence of Pythagoras extended in two directions. His idea that numbers underpin the structure of reality anticipated more modern attempts to understand the universe in terms of mathematics and science. Thus, for example, in *The Republic*, Plato noted that there was a style of living that was deemed Pythagorean, and it involved an interest in philosophy, mathematics, music, and astronomy. In an entirely different direction, the influence of Pythagoras is seen in various attempts to link religious belief to an ideal realm of mathematical perfection.

Metempsychosis: The notion that after a person's death their soul passes into the body of another person or animal. It seems certain that Pythagoras was committed to this belief in the transmigration of souls. Xenophanes famously ridiculed him for claiming to be able to recognize the voice of a friend in the yelping of a puppy.

Socrates

When Cicero said that Socrates was "the first to call philosophy down from the heavens," he meant that in contrast to earlier thinkers such as Parmenides and Anaximander, Socrates' concerns were those of normal life, particularly with regard to the question of how it is best lived. Unfortunately, it is not easy to get a grip on Socrates' thinking, because he didn't write things down for us. Instead we rely almost entirely on the writings of Xenophon and particularly on the early dialogues of Plato for our knowledge of his thoughts and actions.

Born: Ca. 470 BC, Athens, Greece
Importance: Established the Socratic method of argumentation
Died: Ca. 399 BC, Athens, Greece

In fact, we learn more from Plato's dialogues about Socrates' *mode* of philosophizing than we do about his specific views. His normal strategy was to approach a person, or a group of people, and then to pose a question about the nature of some concept, perhaps an apparently abstract quality like "justice" or "virtue." He would then challenge the responses of his interlocutors, until inevitably they became confused, and ended up contradicting themselves. This technique of Socratic dialogue is called *elenchus*.

The question of Socrates' motivations is a matter of some scholarly debate. The dialogues never result in a settled definition of the concepts under debate, so one is rarely clear about the specific views that Socrates had on the matters at hand. Indeed, he famously claimed that the only thing he knew was that he didn't know anything. Thus, legend has it that when he heard that the Oracle at Delphi had pronounced that nobody was wiser than Socrates, he was astonished, and immediately tried to prove it wrong by approaching those who had claimed some wisdom in order to question them about the virtues. Through such dialogues, he discovered that both he and the people he spoke to were at base ignorant. However, what set Socrates apart was that he at least realized and acknowledged his ignorance. In a sense, then, the Oracle was right: Socrates' wisdom lay in his self-awareness, in the fact that he openly acknowledged that he knew nothing.

It is possible that Socrates thought that the point of philosophy was simply to philosophize — in other words, that there is something intrinsically valuable in the act of engaging in critical discussion. Indeed, he described himself as a gadfly, all day long questioning and reproaching the citizens of Athens.

In the end, though, he paid a heavy price for his manner of philosophizing. Perhaps inevitably, the Athenian authorities grew tired of his endless questioning, and he was tried

> I am the gadfly which God has attached to the state, and all day long and in all places am always fastening upon you, arousing and persuading and reproaching you.
>
> Socrates in Plato's *Apology*.

and sentenced to death for the crimes of "corrupting the youth" and "not believing in the city gods." Having insisted that his friends and family should not plead for his life, Socrates met his death precisely as we might expect. He consumed the hemlock which was to kill him, and then calmly engaged with his friends in philosophical discussion.

Plato

Plato's philosophical output was vast and comprehensive, which makes it difficult to treat in summary form. Nevertheless, it is possible to identify a common thread that runs through much of it, which is the notion that there exists a realm of ideal forms.

Plato came to this view through his reflections on the nature of knowledge. He argued that we cannot have genuine knowledge of the temporary and changing world of our everyday lives.

Born: Ca. 427 BC, Athens, Greece
Importance: The father of philosophy
Died: Ca. 347 BC, Athens, Greece

Consider, for example, what it means to claim that something has the color red. At first thought it might seem obvious that, say, our book has a red cover. But what about when we look at it in a darkened room? We might still see the cover as red, but it certainly looks different than it would in sunlight. And what about when it fades a little? Is it still red, and if so why, given that it is a different color than it was previously? Or, to take a different example, consider what it means to say that an animal is a dog. Clearly, dogs are usually four legged, furry creatures. But what if the dog loses a leg? Is it still a dog? How about if it loses its teeth and tail? What exactly is it that constitutes the essence of a dog?

It was these kinds of thoughts that led Plato to the view that knowledge can only ever be of perfect, eternal truths. To satisfy this requirement, to explain how true knowledge is possible, he posited the existence of a realm of ideal forms. These are unchanging, stable, ideal entities, of which the things in the world are merely shadowy copies. Thus, there exists a perfect form of the color red, dogs, stag beetles, and every other extant entity.

Plato's theory of forms, however, extends beyond simple material things to include abstract concepts such as "justice,"

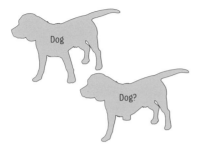

Left: What makes a dog a dog? The number of legs it has? According to Plato, it is because it reflects its equivalent in the realm of perfect forms. It is but a shadowy copy of the perfect form of a dog.

"beauty," and "good." He believed that these too had their equivalents in the realm of the forms. Thus, things in our everyday world are just or beautiful because they partake of the form of justice or beauty.

Although we will never be able to perceive these forms directly, Plato did believe that we could come to an understanding of them. It is here that the philosopher has a role to play, for it is through the exercise of reason that we can gain knowledge of the realm of the forms.

This led Plato to the view which he articulated in the *Republic* that the ideal state is one that is ruled over by philosopher kings. Of all people, they are best placed to achieve true knowledge and wisdom.

There will be no end to the troubles of states, or indeed, my dear Glaucon, of humanity itself, till philosophers become kings in this world, or till those we now call kings and rulers really and truly become philosophers.

Plato *The Republic*

Aristotle

Aristotle, a student of Plato's Academy, is the most modern of the ancient philosophers. He was the first to insist that the pursuit of knowledge should be divided into different areas determined by their focus of enquiry. Thus, for example, he distinguished between natural philosophy, roughly speaking, what we now call science, and metaphysics, what we now call philosophy. He was also the first philosopher to insist on the importance of systematic empirical enquiry and data collection, thus providing the impetus for the development of a kind of scientific method.

Born: 384 BC, Stagira, Macedonia, Greece
Importance: Set the terms of philosophical debate for nearly two millennia
Died: 322 BC, Chalcis, Euboea, Greece

Aristotle's interest in the workings of the material world was indicative of his general philosophical approach. In contrast to Plato, who claimed that our everyday world of experience is but a shadowy copy of the realm of perfect forms, Aristotle believed that ultimate reality resides in physical objects, which it is possible to get to know by observation. Thus, he undertook extensive biological studies, examining more than five hundred species of animals. Although he got much wrong — for example, he believed that the activity of thinking was centered around the heart, and not in the brain — he also made contributions which prefigured later advancements in our understanding of the living world. Perhaps most impressively, he invented a system for the classification of animals that anticipated the Linnaean system, which emerged some two thousand years later.

Perhaps because of his interest in the living world, Aristotle thought that it was possible to explain the existence of things in terms of their functions; that is, in terms of the role that they play

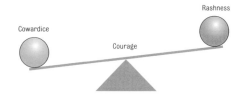

Above: Aristotle's doctrine of the mean holds that any given virtue lies between two extremes, one involving deficiency, the other, excess. Thus, the virtue of courage lies between cowardice (deficiency) and rashness (excess).

in attaining certain goals. Thus, for example, an animal has lungs *in order* to draw air down toward the heart, where it is heated up, and then turned into *pneuma*, the vital life force of the body. Extending this analysis to human beings, it was Aristotle's view that we are constituted by certain internal principles which suggest that our natural function is to reason.

This general idea is also related to his thinking about ethics. A thing is virtuous to the extent that it fulfils its latent potential. Thus, human beings achieve excellence if they act in accordance with the dictates of reason. This led Aristotle to his famous doctrine of the mean. Human beings behave well if they avoid both excess and inappropriate moderation in their responses to the situations that confront them. There is no formula to determine precisely which actions are right on any particular occasion; it is rather a matter of carefully weighing appropriate responses in the light of particular circumstances.

This brief outline of Aristotle's thought barely scratches the surface of his contribution to philosophy. His work in the fields of logic, metaphysics, politics, ethics, biology, and psychology, among others, even today continues to inform the terms of philosophical debate.

Augustine

St. Augustine of Hippo believed that babies who died without having been baptized would suffer the torments of hellfire for eternity. He also thought that sex, even within marriage, was something to be avoided unless absolutely necessary for the purposes of procreation; the problem with sex, he argued, is that it involves a subjugation of the will to the demands of lust, and therefore violates the injunction that virtuous people should at all times be the subjects of their own will.

Born: 354, Tagaste, Numidia (now in Algeria)
Importance: After St Paul, the most significant of the fathers of the Christian church
Died: 430, Hippo Regius (now in Algeria)

Augustine's rather austere theology was rooted in a particular conception of the creation and the fall of man. It was his view that Adam had been created with free will; consequently, it was within his power to have abstained from sin. However, he chose not to, and, as a result, fell into corruption. The curse of mankind is that we have inherited this original sin, and, therefore, we are corrupt through and through. Thus, there are no grounds for complaint if we are condemned to eternal hell, because we deserve it.

> Give me chastity and continence, but not yet.
>
> Augustine *Confessions*

Significantly, Augustine did not think that everybody was destined to go to hell. By the grace of God, a select few from among the baptized will be saved. However, there is an important caveat here. It is not within our power to do anything to achieve God's grace. Augustine did not believe that one could earn one's place in heaven by kind deeds or a virtuous life; humans are inherently depraved, and that is all there is to it. However, God, by virtue of his goodness, chooses to bestow his grace upon an elect few, and they, empowered by grace to follow the ways of God, will, upon their deaths, go to heaven.

Bertrand Russell, in his great history of Western philosophy, pointed out that there is something curious about Augustine's theology of predestination. It apparently doesn't worry Augustine too much that God created mankind knowing that the vast majority of people are predestined to eternal damnation. Yet Augustine does worry that the doctrine of original sin requires that the soul, the locus of sin, as well as the body, is inherited from the parents. Augustine admits that he isn't able to solve this conundrum, so he leaves it up in the air. Russell comments that given Augustine's preoccupations and those of the other great intellects of his time, it is not surprising "that the succeeding age surpassed almost all other fully historical periods in cruelty and superstition."

There is no denying that in terms of his influence on Christian thinking, Augustine has almost unparalleled significance. However, the austerity and unforgiving nature of his theology make him a very difficult person to admire, even allowing for the fact that he lived at a time when different standards prevailed.

Free will: A slippery concept which normally involves the claim that it is possible for humans to make choices that are genuinely undetermined. Thus, a necessary condition of a free choice is that it might not have occurred given the existence of the same precise circumstances under which it was in fact made.

Thomas Aquinas

The great medieval theologian Thomas Aquinas believed that it was possible — indeed, desirable — to reconcile faith and reason. Although the revealed truths of religion were authoritative, it was not, he thought, possible simply to discount knowledge that had been attained by Aristotelian methods of rational inquiry. Therefore, it was necessary to show that religion is supported by reason; that there are good reasons, independent of faith, for believing the truths set out in the Bible.

Born: Ca.1225, Roccasecca, modern-day Italy
Importance: Showed how religious belief might be founded on reason
Died: 1274, Fossanuova, modern-day Italy

Perhaps the best example of Aquinas's desire to work within the framework of reason is to be found in the Five Ways (*quinque viae*), his attempt to prove the existence of God on the basis of arguments about motion, causation, contingency, perfection, and purpose. His Second Way, for example, holds that the world is characterized by definite causal relations. If I use a stick to move a stone, then the stone is caused to move by the stick, which in turn is caused to be moved by my hand, and so on. In this chain of events, there are no uncaused causes; rather there are effects of previous causes, which then become causes themselves. However, the crucial point is that this backward chain of causality cannot continue indefinitely. At some point there must be an uncaused cause — the thing which started the whole chain of causes in the first place. According to Aquinas, this uncaused cause is God.

Although at first glance this argument might seem plausible, it is not, in fact, decisive. Even if one grants that a chain of causes cannot extend back indefinitely (which is a moot point), it just isn't obvious that the uncaused, first cause is the kind of thing which we'd want to call God. Certainly, there is no good reason

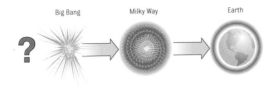

Big Bang   Milky Way   Earth

Above: What caused the Big Bang? And was this cause itself caused? If Aquinas is right, at the beginning of the chain we must eventually find something that is not itself caused. This is God.

to believe that it is the God of the Christian Bible — omnipotent, omniscient, and benevolent. Indeed, it is generally accepted by philosophers and theologians that Aquinas's Five Ways are not decisive in proving the existence of God. Nevertheless, they remain an important demonstration of the way in which reason can be harnessed in order to support religious belief.

It is important to recognize that Aquinas did not think that reason could lead us to a complete knowledge of God. Although we have the ability to come to understand the physical world, we are too limited to know God fully. The knowledge which we do attain, therefore, is incomplete, and comes to us indirectly by means of analogy and negation.

Aquinas was hugely influential. His followers, the Thomists, played a major role in the development of Christian theology. Perhaps most significantly, Aquinas showed that religious belief does not have to be irrational; that even if faith is ultimately the measure of truth, there is still plenty of room left for philosophical argument.

Early Thought

Metaphysics

Charles Bowen, a nineteenth-century British judge, is said to have characterized a metaphysician as "a blind man in a dark room — looking for a black cat, which isn't there." In a similar vein, F. H. Bradley suggested that metaphysics is "the finding of bad reasons for what we believe on instinct ..." It is partly the subject matter of metaphysics that has led to these rather acerbic judgments about its merits. Metaphysics deals with the nature of ultimate reality, a subject so elusive as to leave plenty of room for philosophical flights of fancy. Under its rubric, philosophers since Aristotle have mused about the existence of God, the nature of time, the reality of causality, the nature of being, and other similar topics.

What they say about these things varies. Consider, for example, how philosophers tackle the nature of being. Materialists think that all extant entities are made up of matter or are an attribute of matter. Thus, for example, a strict materialist will deny that mental phenomena — for example, pain — exist at all. Idealist philosophers take precisely the opposite view. They believe that reality, in some sense, comprises mind; that what we take to be the material world actually has a mental character, or, at the very least, is dependent on mind. Thus, for example, George Berkeley claimed that the world is nothing more than an idea in the mind of God.

> When he to whom one speaks does not understand, and he who speaks himself does not understand, that is metaphysics.
>
> Voltaire *Philosophical Dictionary*

It is should be clear then why some people are suspicious of metaphysics. The thought that tables and chairs are made of mind, for example, is highly counterintuitive. The general point is that metaphysicians tend to indulge in speculation which is not based on evidence. Much of this speculation is *a priori* in nature; that is, it makes little, if any, reference to experience. There are two particular worries with this sort of approach. The first is that it encourages the kind of fanciful system-building that is characteristic of the work of philosophers like Hegel. The second, perhaps more significant, worry is the suspicion that if metaphysical statements lack evidential grounding, then they also lack meaning. This criticism is associated with logical positivist philosophers such as A. J. Ayer. It was their claim that meaningful statements are either true as a matter of logic or verifiable by experience. Using these criteria, it is fairly easy to show that many metaphysical statements are in fact meaningless, as Ayer famously did with Bradley's claim that "The Absolute enters into, but is itself incapable of, evolution and progress."

Causality: Denotes a causal relationship between two events, where the occurrence of one (*the cause*) in some way results in the occurrence of the other (*the effect*). The precise nature of causality is a matter of ongoing philosophical debate.

However, despite the problems that metaphysics has faced, it has enjoyed something of a renaissance in recent decades. In part, this is a consequence of the decline of the importance of logical positivism; but it is also thanks to the fact that the nature of metaphysics itself has changed — no doubt partly in response to the criticisms which it faced — and it is now a much more grounded discipline than in the past.

Thomas Hobbes

Thomas Hobbes had a deeply pessimistic view of human nature. In a "state of nature," without the civilizing force of society and political obligation, there is "no knowledge of the face of the earth; no account of time; no arts; no letters; no society; and which is worst of all, continual fear, and danger of violent death; and the life of man, solitary, poor, nasty, brutish, and short."

Born: 1588, Westport, England
Importance: Originated the social contract theory of the State
Died: 1679, Hardwick, England

He came to this view on the grounds that the state of nature is governed by the same kinds of inexorable laws as is the physical world. Thus, with no curbs on the freedoms of people in a state of nature, conflict is inevitable; indeed, absolute freedom means that people are quite at liberty to kill other human beings, if, in some way, it furthers their ends.

There is, however, a way out of this situation — one which surely any rational person will take. People have to give up their absolute freedom, and instead be content with as much liberty in their actions toward other men as they would allow other men to have toward themselves. This requires that all those who seek protection sign up to a "social contract," which in effect transfers absolute freedom from all people to a single person — or group — who then uses this power to keep the peace and ensure the security of all.

It is as if every man should say to every other, "I authorize and give up my right of governing myself to this man or assembly of men, on this condition, that thou give up thy right to him, and authorize all his actions in like manner."

Hobbes argued that the power of any sovereign has to be absolute; it is only this which guarantees protection against the horrors of a state of nature. Thus, the social contract brings into existence "that great LEVIATHAN, or rather, to speak more reverently…that mortal God, to which we owe under the immortal God, our peace and defence."

There are obviously problems with this conception. Most particularly, the idea of investing absolute power in a single person is a little troubling. The philosopher John Locke, for example, pointed out that it isn't clear that the best way to defend ourselves against other humans is by investing power in a super-powerful human being. Thus, Locke wonders whether men are "so foolish that they take care to avoid what mischiefs may be done them by polecats or foxes, but are content, nay think it safety, to be devoured by lions?"

Hobbes's ideas, nevertheless, have been tremendously influential. For example, the notion that human nature is in lots of ways corrupt is one that is accepted by many conservative political philosophers.

Whilst few people today would argue that society should be founded upon the absolute power of a single person, lots would accept that a social contract of the kind envisaged by Locke is both desirable and necessary.

State of nature: An imaginary situation characterized by the absence of both government and the varieties of social constraint that are typical of extant societies.

René Descartes

In his youth, René Descartes was troubled by the lack of certainty attached to the beliefs that he held. Indeed, he reports that eventually he came to the view that "nowhere in the world was there any knowledge professed of the kind I had been encouraged to expect." He was not, however, content to let this situation rest. Rather, he set out to find the bedrock upon which all knowledge might be founded.

Born: 1596, La Haye, France
Importance: Attempted to establish the indubitable basis of knowledge
Died: 1650, Stockholm, Sweden

In his *Meditations on First Philosophy*, he makes use of a method of radical doubt with the aim of establishing at least one certain belief. Descartes' argument here is one of the most famous in the history of philosophy. His technique was to examine his beliefs, and then to cast aside any one of them which it was possible to doubt. In this way, he succeeded in showing that we might be mistaken about a particular sense datum; that it is possible to throw the whole of our sense experience into doubt — we could, for example, be dreaming, yet fail to realize it; and, most troublingly, that it is possible that there is nothing at all behind our experiences of the world — we might merely have been deceived about it all by an evil demon.

However, this method also shows that there is one belief we cannot doubt; namely, that we exist. Descartes' argument here is that the very act of doubting demonstrates there must be an "I" which is doing the doubting. Thus, his famous *Cogito ergo sum* ("I am thinking, therefore, I exist").

However, this argument leads to further problems. First, Descartes sees it as committing him to a metaphysical dualism; that is, he is led to argue that "mind," a thinking substance, is a different kind of thing to the physical body. This results in huge

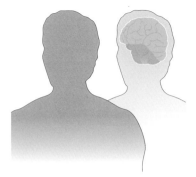

Left: Descartes argued that "mind," a thinking substance, is a different kind of thing to the physical body. The resulting problem has troubled philosophers ever since: how does the mind — the "ghost in the machine" — interact with the body?

philosophical problems, not least how the two kinds of thing interact with each other. It isn't clear, for example, how the mind might instruct the body to move. Second, having established the existence of a thinking entity, it is not easy to get the rest of the world back. His attempt involves employing a version of the "ontological argument" in order to demonstrate the existence of God, and then to argue that since God is not a deceiver, we are not systematically misled about those things we perceive clearly with our senses. It is then fairly easy to get back certain of our beliefs about the external world. However, it is not a persuasive argument; indeed, most modern philosophers would argue that it is deeply flawed.

Descartes' legacy to philosophy has two aspects. He showed how a distinctively philosophical method might be employed with the purpose of establishing fundamental truths about the world; yet in doing so he ushered in a skepticism about truth which philosophy still struggles with to this day.

Baruch Spinoza

It has been said of Baruch Spinoza that he was courteous and reasonable, never bullying, and always seeking to reason with his adversaries rather than vilify them. It is hardly fitting then that he spent his life struggling with the effects of a religious intolerance that sought to condemn him. The source of his difficulties was his unorthodox religious beliefs; his pantheism, the belief that God is present in everything, just didn't go down too well in seventeenth-century Europe.

Born: 1632, Amsterdam, Netherlands
Importance: A beacon for religious freedom in an age of sectarian intolerance
Died: 1677, The Hague, Netherlands

Spinoza set out his ideas about God and Nature in *Ethica*, one of the great works of Western philosophy. He argued that reality comprises just one substance, which can be conceived of as either God or Nature; God did not create the universe, but rather is identical with it. It was Spinoza's view that everything which occurs in reality is a necessary manifestation of the Divinity. Thus, there is no room in his scheme for free will. Indeed, he argued that to believe in free will is to dream with one's eyes open; it is only because we are ignorant of the real causes of our actions that we are able to sustain such a conceit.

> Men are deceived if they think themselves free, an opinion which consists only in this, that they are conscious of their actions and ignorant of the causes by which they are determined.
>
> Spinoza *Ethica*

Spinoza's thoroughgoing determinism has implications for ideas to do with evil, sin, and the possibility of damnation, three of the staples of orthodox Christian theology. In particular, determinism undercuts the idea of moral responsibility. If a murderer is *necessarily* a murderer, then how is he blameworthy? Moreover, if reality, in all its forms, is identical to God, how can a murderer, an aspect of reality, be evil? Spinoza's answer to this question was that from the point of view of God, there is no evil in sin; human beings only see evil in the world because they have limited knowledge; like Leibniz after him, Spinoza thought that our ignorance of ultimate reality precludes us from seeing evil in its proper aspect.

Despite his rejection of the idea of free will, Spinoza did have something to say about how people should live their lives. It was his belief that humans should strive to see reality as God sees it; that is, from the *perspective of eternity*. If we can do this, and thereby see how small our troubles are in comparison to the majesty of Nature, then we achieve a sort of freedom. Recognizing our place in the larger whole, and seeing its goodness, we set ourselves free from those of our passions, like the fear of death, which are based upon human finitude.

Bertrand Russell suggested that in a painful world our ability to see our troubles from the perspective of the whole of reality is "a help towards sanity and an antidote to the paralysis of utter despair." If he is right, then Spinoza's ethical message is as pertinent today as it was three hundred years ago.

Determinism: In its most general sense, determinism asserts that all events are effects of other events which are themselves effects of other events, and so on. If it is true, it leads to the troubling thought that all human choices might be effects — that is, that they are caused — so that people cannot act in any way other than they do.

John Locke

Some philosophers make much of what are called "innate ideas" — ideas which exist in our minds that have not been derived from experience. Plato, for example, thought that all ideas were like this; we do not learn new things, so much as remember what we already know. And Descartes suggested that our idea of God, amongst others, was innate (or, if not, it had been planted in our minds by God himself). It was against the possibility of innate ideas that John Locke deployed his brilliant *Essay Concerning Human Understanding*.

Born: 1632, Wrington, England
Importance: Developed the "blank slate" view of the human mind
Died: 1704, Oates, England

The position that Locke outlined in this work has come to be known as empiricism, the doctrine that all our knowledge is derived from experience, through the action of the physical world upon our senses. It was Locke's view that we are born with minds like blank slates (*tabula rasa*), which are then written on by the world of experience. Specifically, sensory experience generates "simple ideas," which are "nothing but one uniform appearance or conception in the mind." In addition, our mind is able to construct "complex ideas" by combining and shifting its store of simple ideas.

Perhaps the key point here is the claim that we have knowledge of ideas, not of the objects to which these ideas apparently refer. Thus, Locke argued that: "Since the mind, in all its thoughts and reasonings, hath no other immediate object but its own ideas...it is evident that our knowledge is only conversant about them."

Unfortunately, this notion creates huge problems. If knowledge is of ideas that exist purely in the mind, then it seems that we've been shunted off into a closet from which we cannot escape. Locke is not able to argue, without pain of inconsistency, that there are good grounds for supposing that our ideas correspond to things in the world, because this requires the kind of *a priori* (or innate) knowledge which his framework does not allow. This is a problem that has troubled empiricism from the start, and it hasn't been solved to this day. Locke's view seems to lead directly to skepticism about the possibility of knowledge.

Locke's account also suffers in modern terms from what we have come to know about the mind. The blank slate view just isn't plausible; particularly, with the emergence of disciplines such as sociobiology and evolutionary psychology, we are now able to show that there are indeed aspects of our knowledge which, in a certain sense at least, are innate.

Nevertheless, Locke's influence and importance is undeniable. He set the terms of debate for an awful lot of modern philosophy, and many people consider him to be right up there with David Hume as Britain's greatest philosopher.

Empiricism: The thesis that genuine knowledge about the world is derived from the senses. In its scientific form, empiricism results in a commitment to the importance of experiment, observation, and measurement.

Left: Locke's empiricist view holds that all knowledge is ultimately based on the experiences that are written onto the "blank slates" of our minds.

Philosophical Thought

Epistemology

From the very earliest days of philosophy, there have been worries about whether it is possible to know anything; and also that if things are known, whether it will be clear that they are known. Socrates, for example, famously insisted that he didn't know anything, but that at least he *knew* that he didn't know anything. And Protagoras, the most famous of the sophists, made his reputation largely on the basis of his claim that "man is the measure of all things," by which he meant, roughly speaking, that all beliefs are true from the perspective of the person asserting the belief.

Protagoras's view is an early example of relativism; that is, the idea that things are true or false only from particular perspectives. The responses which his claim provoked all those years ago are indicative of the way that philosophers down the ages have tried to deal with what they see as the threat of relativism. First, his critics attempted to show that the statement was self-refuting. If all beliefs are true from someone's perspective, then it follows that the belief that all beliefs are *not* true from someone's perspective must be true, which means that the claim that all beliefs are true from someone's perspective can't be true. A paradox. Unfortunately, this argument was itself easily refuted. The relativist does not universalize truth-claims; in other words, their claim is merely that beliefs are true for the people who hold them, not that they are true for everybody.

> Man is the measure of all things.
>
> Protagoras *Fragment 1*

However, this opens the relativist up to a much more powerful objection. If the claim is that beliefs are true for everybody only in the limited sense that any particular belief is true for the person who asserts it, then it is an empty claim. Indeed, it isn't clear that it is even meaningful to make such a claim; the idea that something can be "true" for just one person, seems to do violence to the idea of truth.

Relativism, and its cousin skepticism, have not, however, gone away. Thinkers in the early modern period such as Montaigne were troubled by them, after they became aware that people live very different lives in the New World; philosophers in the eighteenth and nineteenth century were worried about the implications for skepticism of Descartes' project to find the indubitable foundations of knowledge, and also of Locke's idea that knowledge is rooted in sense impressions which come in from the outside world. Subsequently, philosophers in the twentieth century became concerned about the role which language plays in our understanding of the world, with whether, in fact, truth-claims are relative to particular discourses or "language-games," and, more radically, whether language refers to nothing in the world at all.

Epistemology, then, as the branch of philosophy concerned with knowledge, is frequently an exercise in firefighting, concerned not so much with what we know, as with refuting the claim that we know nothing at all.

Sophists: A group of early Greek philosophers — including Protagoras, who crops up in a number of Plato's dialogues — who perhaps unfairly are known for their ability to argue for any position, using their skills in logic and rhetoric, regardless of its truth or falsity. Thus, the term "sophistry" refers to the use of argument in order to bamboozle or confuse.

George Berkeley

It is possible to play a nice little visual trick in order to show that there is a difference between the world as it appears to us and the world itself. Close one eye; then place a finger on the edge of your other eye, and gently nudge your eyeball backward and forward. You'll find that everything shifts from side to side. Unless the world has suddenly started to move in a bizarre way, the only possible conclusion seems to be that what we see is not the world itself, but a representation of it. This immediately leads to a difficult problem. How do we know that our representation of the world corresponds to the real world?

Born: 1685, County Kilkenny, Ireland
Importance: Held that objects only exist through being perceived
Died: 1753, Oxford, England

George Berkeley's solution to this problem was simply to deny that the material world exists outside our minds. "That the things I see with my eyes and touch with my hands exist, really exist, I make not the least question. The only thing whose existence we deny is that which philosophers call Matter or corporeal substance." He argued instead that all objects exist through being perceived; or, as he put it, "to be is to be perceived." Berkeley employed a series of arguments to demonstrate his

... those difficulties which have hitherto amused philosophers, and blocked up the way to knowledge, are entirely owing to ourselves. We have first raised a dust, and then complain we cannot see.

Berkeley *Principles of Human Knowledge*

immaterialism. For example, to show that heat is purely a mental phenomenon, he noted that if one of our hands is cold, and the other hot, and we put them both into warm water, the water seems hot to one hand, and cold to the other. Since water cannot be both these things together, it shows that "heat and cold are only sensations existing in our minds."

Heat and cold are examples of what John Locke called the "secondary qualities" of an object, which are indeed mind-dependent. But what about things like motion and shape, and the other "primary qualities," which are mind-independent? Surely they exist outside the mind? Berkeley's argument is that the distinction between primary and secondary qualities is an illusion. It is just impossible to think of the shape of an object, for example, without also giving it a quality such as color, which exists only in the mind, thereby showing that the so-called primary qualities are themselves dependent on the mind.

Immaterialism: The notion that the world has no physical reality, but that it exists rather in the mind as perceptions or ideas.

Perhaps the major puzzle associated with Berkeley's idea is how objects persist if they are not being perceived. After all, it would be absurd to think, as you read this book, that the world behind your head no longer exists; but surely this is what Berkeley's idea entails? Berkeley's response was to argue that all our ideas — indeed the entire world of sensible experience — are an effect of the power of God. God is all-seeing, and thereby He brings the world of ideas into existence.

Berkeley's philosophy is clearly highly counterintuitive. However, in order to show where he went wrong, it requires a lot more than merely kicking a stone, as Samuel Johnson was said to have done in order to refute Berkeley.

David Hume

David Hume is perhaps the greatest philosopher in the skeptical tradition. Indeed, Bertrand Russell claims that it isn't really possible to get past Hume; you can't refute his arguments, yet there remains a wish that something a little less skeptical than his system might one day be discovered.

Born: 1711, Edinburgh, Scotland
Importance: His ideas are the culmination of the empirical, skeptical tradition
Died: 1776, Edinburgh, Scotland

Hume's skepticism was, indeed, far reaching. He questioned, for example, the existence of miracles, God, the logic of causation, and the possibility of inductive knowledge (roughly speaking, knowledge based on evidence). Perhaps more disconcertingly, he also suggested that we were not justified in believing in an enduring, permanent self; in other words, he rejected our common notion of personal identity.

The issue of personal identity is this: We tend to think that we are the same person as we were say ten years ago. We also think that in ten years time we'll be the same person as we are now. Of course, we recognize that over time our attitudes and opinions change, and maybe even our personalities, but nevertheless we suppose that something pretty fundamental endures, and whatever it is, it is what defines us as us. Hume realizes that we have this picture of personal identity, but he can find nothing to justify the idea. When he introspects — that is, turns his attention to his sense impressions — all he can find is a constantly changing "bundle of perceptions," but no enduring "self." Hume therefore contends that the idea of the self is a convenient fiction.

Hume's ideas about the self are certainly disconcerting; however, perhaps the skeptical argument which has most troubled philosophers is the attack he made on the way we traditionally think about causality.

It was Hume's view that there is nothing in the world which adds up to logically necessary causal relationships. If one billiard ball strikes another, which then moves, we will tend to say that the first ball has caused the movement (the effect) of the second. According to Hume, this is an inference — we've seen this kind of thing many times before, so we assume that the world will manifest the same cause and effect conjunction in the future. But the key point is that there is nothing which justifies this conjunction logically. It is quite conceivable that on any particular occasion the ball being struck will not move; there is nothing about its behavior in the past which necessitates future behavior. Thus, according to Hume, it is not reason, but habit which leads us to expect that like causes will produce like effects; in the end, only human nature underpins our thinking in this connection.

Although Hume's skepticism casts an enduring shadow over philosophy, by many people's reckoning he is the greatest of the modern philosophers; and perhaps also the philosopher most read, and thought about, in the Western analytic tradition.

Immanuel Kant

According to empiricist philosophers in the mold of John Locke, the mind is "white paper, void of all characters," upon which experiences are written as they come in from the outside world. The idea then is that to the extent that the experiences written there represent the world, we have knowledge of it. However, there is a problem with this idea: knowledge seems to require the sort of conceptual content which sense impressions cannot supply.

Born: 1724, Königsberg, Prussia (now Kaliningrad, Russia)
Importance: Sought to reconcile the rationalist and empiricist traditions
Died: 1804, Königsberg, Prussia

It was Immanuel Kant, more than anybody, who made this clear. In his great work *Critique of Pure Reason*, he distinguished between a "noumenal world," the world of things in themselves, and the "phenomenal world," the world of appearances. He argued that while the nature of the objects of the noumenal world "remains completely unknown to us," we can know something of the phenomenal world.

> You might just take Bertrand Russell on a beach holiday, as I once did; but Kant, never.
>
> Simon Blackburn
> *The New Republic*

The key point is that the mind shapes, categorizes, and organizes the experiences that constitute the phenomenal world; in other words, it imposes order on the raw data which come in from our senses. Specifically, experiences are organized by our minds in terms of the concepts of space and time, and on the basis of a number of further categories of understanding, which include cause/effect and substance. Thus, to take the example of space, Kant claimed that the world in itself, the noumenal world, does not have spatial relationships. Rather, the spatial properties of the phenomenal world are imposed on the raw data of our sense experience by our minds. In other words, we represent the world to ourselves as spatial.

It was by means of this general argument, which he thought amounted to a "Copernican revolution," that Kant attempted to solve the problem of the conceptual underpinning of knowledge, and more generally to show how it is possible to attain knowledge from sense experience alone. In essence, Kant's claim was that by the mechanism of a number of "forms of intuition," the mind plays an active role in shaping and structuring the knowable world.

However, there are, of course, problems attached to Kant's account. Not least, his distinction between raw sense data and the conceptual operations of the mind threatens relativism, because of the possibility — which he rejected — that different minds might organize the world in different ways. Moreover, some philosophers have found the idea that there is an aspect of reality — the noumenal world — which is forever out of our reach unpalatable.

The scope of Kant's philosophy extends well beyond the concerns which have been outlined here. He also did groundbreaking work in the areas of ethics and aesthetics, and on issues such as free will and causality. Indeed, he is almost universally considered to be the greatest Enlightenment philosopher, and many people consider him also to have been the greatest modern philosopher.

Relativism: Relativism has many different forms. Moral relativism, for example, asserts that moral judgments are true or false only from the perspective of particular cultures or discourses. Epistemological relativism makes the same claim for knowledge about the world; that is, that statements about the nature of the world are true or false only relative to particular social and/or linguistic contexts.

Georg F. Hegel

G. F. Hegel's most important work of philosophy, *The Phenomenology of Spirit*, is almost impossible to understand. Indeed, his prose style is so complex and convoluted that some people have suspected that he was a philosophical charlatan.

However, it is more likely that the complexity of his work is a function of the enormity of the task that he set for himself, which was to chart the unfolding of Being, or Absolute Spirit, across the whole of history.

Born: 1770, Stuttgart, modern-day Germany
Importance: The last of the great, metaphysical system-builders
Died: 1831, Berlin, modern-day Germany

Hegel's philosophy rests on a system of dialectical reasoning. This is best understood in terms of the concepts of *thesis*, *antithesis*, and *synthesis*. Put simply, the idea is that any given phenomenon (*thesis*) contains within itself contradictory aspects (*antithesis*) that require a movement toward resolution (*synthesis*) and that progress in our understanding of reality occurs according to a process that has this dialectical form. It is possible to illustrate this idea by looking at Hegel's famous dialectic of master and slave.

It was Hegel's view that a self-consciousness exists — or human beings, as self-conscious beings, exist — to the extent that it is recognized as self-conscious by another self-consciousness. However, Hegel argued that this kind of mutual recognition between self-consciousnesses will not be easily won. At first, neither self-consciousness is certain of the self-consciousness of the other, and hence both are deprived of the source of their own certainty. Consequently, each will try to attain the recognition of the other without reciprocating.

According to Hegel, the struggle for one-sided recognition which results is necessarily to the death, because only in risking

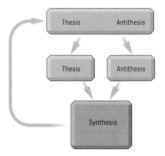

Left: Hegel's idea was that any given phenomenon (thesis) contains within itself a contradictory aspect (antithesis). Tension between the two is resolved only through a movement to a new situation (a synthesis), whose own instability leads to the whole process starting again.

their own lives can these self-consciousnesses demonstrate to each other, and to themselves, their freedom from their particular bodily forms, and hence their status as *beings for themselves*. However, it is clear that in this context, the death of either participant would be irrelevant, since it would deprive the survivor of recognition altogether. Hence, the solution, to a struggle which must put the life of each participant in danger, is the enslavement of one and the mastery of the other.

> The one is independent, and its essential nature is to be for itself; the other is dependent, and its essence is life or existence for another. The former is the Master, or Lord, the latter the Bondsman.

However, it was Hegel's view that the opposition between individuals is something which will in time be overcome. The dialectic of master and slave is simply one of the phases which self-consciousness must pass through on its way to self-certainty.

Hegel's ideas were hugely influential throughout the nineteenth century. However, since then, his kind of philosophy — namely, the tradition which is fond of grand metaphysical speculation — has fallen on hard times. Therefore, it is likely to be quite a while before we see another philosopher in the mold of Hegel.

Philosophical Thought

Søren Kierkegaard

Until Søren Kierkegaard appeared on the scene, philosophy had been in danger of floating off on a cloud of abstract, metaphysical speculation, which, though impressively logical and systematic, was almost entirely divorced from the concerns of human life. Kierkegaard helped to bring philosophy back down to earth again with his insistence that subjectivity, passion, commitment, and faith, and the paradoxes which these bring, are all part of the human situation.

Born: 1813, Copenhagen, Denmark
Importance: Insisted upon the philosophical significance of passion, commitment, and faith
Died: 1855, Copenhagen, Denmark

In denying that it is possible to achieve objective knowledge of the totality of human life and history by the means of a logical and systematic philosophy, Kierkegaard's particular target was Hegelianism, the then dominant philosophical approach in Denmark. With its insistence upon logical necessity, Hegelianism was necessarily flawed; for example, with respect to religion, it aimed to make God and the Christian faith transparent to reason, whereas the reality is that they are necessarily beyond rational understanding.

There are, as is known, insects that die in the moment of fertilization. So it is with all joy: life's highest, most splendid moment of enjoyment is accompanied by death.

Kierkegaard *Either/Or*

In fact, according to Kierkegaard, the religious sphere is constituted by a "leap of faith." It is simply not possible to appeal to rational argument or empirical evidence to justify a belief in the God-man Jesus, who, paradoxically, is both temporal and eternal. All that is available to the believer is a freely chosen commitment to God. In *Fear and Trembling*, Kierkegaard spells out what this might mean for ethics by looking at the biblical story of Abraham and Isaac.

God commands Abraham to kill his son Isaac. To obey this instruction, Abraham must behave in a way that is completely outside the domain of normal morals; it necessitates a "suspension of the ethical" in the service of a higher goal. Abraham must simply follow a command which comes to him from above, one that will have a consequence which in terms of normal morality is completely unacceptable — the murder of his son. Not only can he not justify his actions to other people, he cannot even explain them to himself. All that he has is a felt commitment to God, which is legitimated and authenticated in his obedience.

Religious faith then is not an easy option; indeed, according to Kierkegaard, proper religious faith can only be achieved with great difficulty. So why choose it? The answer is that it is only by religious faith that individuals can avoid despair and dread, and find their true selves in the freedom that, paradoxically, an ongoing commitment to God brings.

Kierkegaard never achieved great recognition for his work during his lifetime. However, with the emergence of existentialism in the twentieth century, which placed the individual at the center of philosophy, the originality of his work is now fully appreciated, and he is rightly considered to be one of the greats of nineteenth-century philosophy.

Morality: Moral claims are based on the idea that behavior can be judged in terms of notions of ought or should. Perhaps what best distinguishes a moral ought (one ought not to hurt other people) from a non-moral ought (one ought not to miss a night's sleep) is that violating a moral ought is felt to be worthy of blame. Thus, something is morally right when one ought to do it, and morally wrong when one ought not to do it, if to behave in a contrary fashion is to warrant sanction.

Friedrich Nietzsche

Friedrich Nietzsche is probably best known for his declaration that "God is dead"; however, what is less well known is that this claim wasn't so much a metaphysical statement of God's non-existence, as a comment on the state of the prevailing system of morals and values in his age. It was his belief that its foundations were disintegrating. We were, he thought, on the edge of a crisis of values, a situation which brought both risks and opportunities. Risks, because without an urgent reinvention of ourselves, we were likely to fall into nihilism and barbarity; but opportunities, because "the horizon seems open once more…our ships can at last put out to sea in face of every danger; every hazard is again permitted to the discerner; the sea, *our* sea, again lies open before us; perhaps never before did such an 'open sea' exist."

Born: 1844, Röcken, Prussia (now Germany)
Importance: Argued for a radical reevaluation of all values
Died: 1900, Weimar, Germany

Nietzsche hoped that by explicating the history and the ideas that underpin our systems of morality, it would be possible to learn enough to undermine them. Thus, he distinguished between a master-morality and a slave-morality. In the former, qualities like power, pride, and truthfulness are valued, thought to be "good," because they exemplify what is best about dominant people.

Morality in Europe today is herd animal morality.

Nietzsche *Beyond Good and Evil*

Conversely, humility, weakness, and timidity are despised, because they are indicative of a kind of slave mentality. However, the enslaved themselves see things differently, and what has occurred, particularly in Christianity, is a reversal of the master-

Left: Nietzsche argued that it is time for us to turn away from the meekness and humility of Christianity's "slave-morality," and instead stake out a place in the world according to humanity's "will to power."

morality. The idea of "good" has become synonymous with weakness, meekness, and suffering, as well as with those qualities which work in the interests of the weak: humility, sympathy, and patience. "Evil," in its turn, has become a term of abuse leveled by the weak at those characteristics of the powerful which they most despise: their health, strength, and power. As a result of this reversal, we now have a slave-morality; and although Nietzsche didn't quite advocate a return to a master-morality, he certainly thought that something like it was required.

His vision of humanity's future found its most succinct expression in the idea of the Superman or Overman. His view was that there is an imperative that human beings as they are now, defined by their crumbling system of values, are "overcome." The figure of the Overman stands for the future of humanity, "the lightning out of the dark cloud of man." His destiny is to renounce the current disintegrating framework of values, and to mark down his own place in the world according to his "will to power."

Nietzsche is a paradoxical philosopher. At the same time, obscure, enigmatic, controversial, yet hugely influential, he is perhaps the most important of all of the philosophers working in what might be called the "continental tradition."

Philosophical Thought

Bertrand Russell

Imagine this: you've devoted the last thirty years of your life to developing a theory of the foundations of mathematics, which you now consider to be complete. You then receive a letter in the post. In it, there is a single argument which wrecks your whole system; your life's work, in effect. This is what happened to the German philosopher Gottlob Frege in 1903. The letter was from Bertrand Russell, and the argument went something like this:

Born: 1872, Trelleck, England
Importance: In his early work, he laid the foundations of modern logic
Died: 1970, Merioneth, Wales

You have just become the head librarian at a huge, old library. One day, whilst exploring, you come across a whole series of catalogs, which detail all the books in the various collections at the library. When you look at the catalogs, you find that they have not been put together consistently. Some of them include themselves as a member of the collection they detail, some of them don't.

You decide that you're going to create a master catalog to list these various catalogs. But then you remember that there are two kinds of catalogs: those which include themselves in their entries, and those which don't, so you determine that two master catalogs is the way to go.

Then you hit a dilemma. You've decided that since the master catalogs are themselves catalogs they should contain themselves in their entries. There is no problem with the first of the two new catalogs — the one that lists all catalogs which include themselves in their entries — since it can just include itself as an entry. But you get stuck with the second of the catalogs — the one which lists all the catalogs which *don't* include themselves in their entries. If it has an entry referring to itself, then it is *not* a catalog which doesn't include itself as an entry, so it *shouldn't* have an

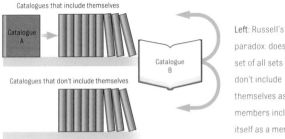

Catalogues that include themselves

Catalogue A

Catalogues that don't include themselves

Catalogue B

Left: Russell's paradox: does the set of all sets which don't include themselves as members include itself as a member?

entry referring to itself. But if it doesn't have an entry referring to itself, then it *is* a catalog which doesn't include itself as an entry, so it *should* have an entry referring to itself. You find out that you're stuck; you've come across a paradox.

In fact, this is a version of what is now known as "Russell's Paradox," the argument which undid Gottlob Frege in 1903. Its more formal expression is as follows: Does the set of all sets which don't include

Mathematics, rightly viewed, possesses not only truth, but supreme beauty — a beauty cold and austere ... yet sublimely pure.

Russell *The Study of Mathematics*

themselves as members, include itself as a member? If it doesn't, then it should; if it does, then it shouldn't. The actual argument is (fairly) straightforward, but its consequences were huge. It showed that there was something wrong with the way that people were thinking about logic and mathematics at the turn of the twentieth century.

Of course, this argument is only a tiny part of Russell's contribution to the way in which we now think about logic. However, it is indicative of the style of his early work; rigorous, forensic, and for Frege, at least, devastating.

Philosophical Thought

Ludwig Wittgenstein

In his posthumously published work, *Philosophical Investigations*, Wittgenstein claimed that philosophy "is a battle against the bewitchment of our intelligence by means of language." The ideas which he developed in his philosophical work were largely employed in the service of this battle; however, it is a striking thing about Wittgenstein's career that he had a radical change of mind about how this battle is best fought.

Born: 1889, Vienna, Austria
Importance: Showed how the structures of language can confuse and mislead
Died: 1951, Cambridge, England

In his *Tractatus Logico-Philosophicus*, his first great work of philosophy, he outlined what has become known as the picture theory of meaning. Put simply, his argument was that the logical structure of language mirrors the structure of reality. Thus, a simple proposition — for example, the cat is on the mat — picks out a possible state of affair of the world. Whether the proposition is true or false depends on whether the state of affair obtains in reality. Wittgenstein argued that statements that were not ultimately reducible to this simple form were nonsense. This included pretty much everything which passed as philosophy; and indeed, according to Wittgenstein, even those statements which comprised the *Tractatus*. The job of philosophy then is to ensure that we don't get mixed up about which statements are meaningful and which are not.

After the publication of the *Tractatus* in 1922, Wittgenstein took a break from philosophy. He started again when he began to suspect that he had got things wrong the first time around. In his later work, he came to the view that language is integrally related to the contexts in which it is used. He argued that words gain their meaning through the rules which govern their usage;

Left: Words gain their meaning from the contexts in which they are employed. Thus, "Quick march!" means something quite different when said by a mother to a toddler than it does when shouted by an officer on a parade ground.

and that different "language-games" are governed by different rules. Thus, for example, "Quick march!" shouted on an army parade ground means something quite different than when a mother says it to her children in the hope that they'll get themselves off to bed quickly.

Wittgenstein's later ideas about language are set out, most significantly, in *Investigations*. He showed here that the project of the *Tractatus* was fundamentally misconceived. Language is not, as he originally thought, a determinate system that can be specified in precise logical terms. Rather, it is a lived practice, which can be employed in an almost limitless number of contexts for a variety of different purposes.

However, although Wittgenstein largely came to reject the arguments of the *Tractatus*, it would be wrong to think that the break between his early and later work was total. Throughout his career he remained committed to the belief that the task of philosophy is to uncover and analyze the various ways in which we are befuddled and misled by language; the project of philosophy, then, is to clarify and dissolve linguistic confusion.

Philosophical Thought

Jean-Paul Sartre

Jean-Paul Sartre is the consummate existentialist philosopher. His work explored all the classic themes of this mode of thinking; particularly, the primacy of individual existence, the character of human freedom, and the nature of ethics.

Born: 1905, Paris, France
Importance: Articulated the definitive theory of existentialism
Died: 1980, Paris, France

Sartre's existentialist philosophy, as outlined in *Being and Nothingness*, started with an analysis of the nature of being. He divided "being" into two primary spheres: being for-itself, which is consciousness; and being in-itself, which is everything else. He argued that the for-itself is characterized by *nothingness*; that is, that emptiness lies right at the center of being. Put simply, he meant by this that there is no human essence; consciousness, detached from the world of things, is pure, empty possibility, and therein lies its freedom.

It is possible to see what this idea involves by considering Sartre's treatment of the concept of "negation." This concerns the ability of individuals to conceive of what is not the case. It is evident in a whole series of attitudes that a conscious being can adopt toward the objects to which it is directed. Perhaps most important is the ability of the for-itself to project beyond the present moment into an open future of unrealized possibilities. In this sense, freedom lies in the permanent possibility that things might be different.

In the face of such radical freedom, human beings experience anguish. Sartre argued that in order to escape such *anguish* people adopt strategies of *bad faith*; that is, they seek to deny the freedom that is inevitably theirs. Thus, for example, a kind of bad faith enters into decisions which people make over matters of morality. The person who claims that they can't have sex before

Still Free

marriage because it is wrong in God's eyes is, in Sartrean terms, guilty of bad faith. There *are* no binding moral codes. All that people can do is to make their choices authentically in the full knowledge that they are choosing freely.

However, Sartre did not think people make choices in a chaotic, random way. There is a certain *facticity* to the situations that individuals confront; choices are made against a particular concrete background which cannot be changed. So people are not free to do absolutely anything. For example, if you're chained to a wall, and a person is pointing a gun at your head, then your freedom of action is *de facto* limited. However, even in this situation you remain fundamentally free. You retain the ability to adopt any attitude you choose toward the situation which you confront. More than this, since human beings are necessarily free, you are compelled to choose how you're going to face up to the possibility of your death.

> Human-reality is free because it is not enough. It is free because it is perpetually wrenched away from itself.
>
> Sartre *Being and Nothingness*

Sigmund Freud

Before Sigmund Freud came along it was easy enough to suppose that human beings were rational decision makers and the masters of their own minds. It is still possible to believe such a thing — just ask a rational choice theorist — but Freud, with his idea that human behavior is driven by a dynamic unconscious over which there is little control, has made it a whole lot harder.

Born: 1856, Freiberg, Moravia, Austrian Empire (now Pribor in the Czech Republic)
Importance: The founder of psychoanalysis
Died: 1939, London, England

Freud argued that the human personality has three distinct aspects: the id, which comprises a person's instincts, primarily, their sexual instincts; the ego, which is the rational, decision-making aspect of the personality; and the superego, which is the moral, censorious part. The id seeks the immediate gratification of its desires; however, formed out of the "reality principle," it is the job of the ego to balance the desires of the id against the demands of living in the world. At the same time, the ego has to keep the superego happy, by ensuring that a person's behavior falls within limits that are morally acceptable from the point of view of the superego.

> The interpretation of dreams is the royal road to a knowledge of the unconscious activities of the mind.
>
> Freud *The Interpretation of Dreams*

This situation is ripe with the potential for psychic conflict. For example, an over-strong superego will result in guilt, anxiety, and a lot of desires and memories buried deep in the unconscious. It was Freud's view that conflicts which are repressed in this manner

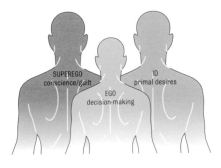

Left: According to Freud, the ego, the rational decision-making part of the self, is caught between the demands of the id and the superego. A person's mental health depends on the ability of their ego to reconcile these inner conflicts.

SUPEREGO
conscience/guilt

ID
primal desires

EGO
decision-making

retain a dynamic character. They are able to make their presence felt in various ways — for instance, in dreams, slips of the tongue, phobias, and fantasy — in the conscious mind. For example, in a famous case study, Freud argued that the fear of horses experienced by Little Hans was in fact a manifestation of his fear of his father, which was rooted in an Oedipal desire for his mother, and the fact that his father was therefore a kind of love rival.

According to Freud, it is the job of the psychoanalyst to unravel the messages which the unconscious sends to the conscious mind. The analyst will employ techniques such as free association, word association, and dream analysis in an attempt to bring repressed memories to the surface. The idea is that by knowing the unconscious roots of our thoughts and behavior we will be in a better position to control them. However, it must be said that there is very little evidence that psychoanalysis has the therapeutic effect that is claimed for it.

It would be hard to overestimate the impact of Freud's ideas on Western thought in the twentieth century. Above all else, he showed that the idea of the rational, autonomous self is a lot more problematic than it might at first seem.

Psychoanalysis

The aim of psychoanalysis, a technique first developed by Sigmund Freud, is to make the "unconscious conscious," and thereby to help patients attain psychological equilibrium. The idea that revealing the unconscious could have therapeutic benefits emerged out of Freud's experience of using hypnosis with clients in the late 1890s. He found that merely by revealing the causes of a person's problems it was possible to bring improvements in their well-being.

Psychoanalysts draw on various mechanisms to access the unconscious minds of their clients. The most significant is perhaps *transference*, which occurs when an "analysand" — the person undergoing psychoanalysis — projects their repressed thoughts, feelings, and desires, particularly those which are rooted in early childhood experiences, onto the therapist, who is then able to help them to come to an understanding of what these mean. This is not an easy process. Freud claimed that transference would always meet resistance, perhaps manifest in things like anger, avoidance, or flippancy, which would itself require further analysis and interpretation.

Although transference is the most important aspect of the therapeutic encounter, it is not the only technique available to the analyst. Freud stressed the importance of free association and the interpretation of dreams. In free association, the client says whatever comes into their head, however silly, irrelevant, or fantastic it might seem. A skilled analyst will then be able to pick up on hesitations, unconscious connections, and the like, in order to help the client to recover lost memories.

Dream interpretation involves treating the client's dreams as symbolic representations of unconscious desires. The idea here is that during sleep the various mechanisms that keep these desires at bay act with much less force than they do during waking hours, thereby allowing the unconscious to make its presence felt in the mind of the dreamer, albeit in a heavily disguised form. The trick is to decode the dream in order to uncover its hidden meaning or, more precisely, its latent content. This involves reversing the "dream work," which has constructed the manifest content of the dream, allowing access to its latent content, and with it the repressed desire that it represents.

Psychoanalysis is only really recommended for people suffering from the less serious personality disorders (e.g., phobias, or mild, but chronic, depression). A person with acute schizophrenia, for example, notwithstanding that we now know that this illness is at least in part a physiological disorder, will rarely be lucid enough for analysis to be useful.

The psychoanalytic encounter is emotionally demanding, time consuming, expensive, and requires a certain level of intellectual competence on the part of the analysand. The big question, of course, is whether it works. There is an argument here about what constitutes "working" in the case of psychoanalysis. While analysts do keep case notes, they are not dealing with easily measurable phenomena, which makes a definitive judgment difficult. Nevertheless, the consensus within the world of psychology, at least, is that the jury is very much out on the therapeutic benefit of psychoanalysis.

Oedipus complex:
Freudian idea, referencing the Greek myth of Oedipus, which holds that young children, particularly sons, seek sexual fulfilment with the parent of the opposite sex. Freud thought that the resolution of the Oedipus complex occurs when the young child ceases to consider the parent of the same sex a sexual rival, but comes instead to identify with them.

Carl Gustav Jung

Carl Jung was a pupil, and then friend, of Sigmund Freud from 1906 until they fell out in 1913. Their break was at least partly caused by Jung's independence of mind, and his desire to take psychoanalytic theory in directions that Freud had not explored.

In particular, Jung rejected the idea that the libido was entirely sexual in character, and, therefore, against Freud, he denied that all neuroses could be understood in terms of sexual conflict.

Born: 1875, Kesswil, Switzerland
Importance: The founder of analytical psychology
Died: 1961, Küsnacht, Switzerland

After the break with Freud, Jung began to develop his own distinctive theory of psychic functioning. He argued that the psyche is split into three separate, but interacting, parts: consciousness; the personal unconscious; and the collective unconscious.

The conscious mind is the aspect of the psyche which is directly known to a person. Jung claimed that there are two personality types that determine how an individual is oriented toward the world. The "extrovert" directs their libidinal energies outward toward the external world. The "introvert," in contrast, is inward looking, concerned with subjective feelings and experience. It was Jung's belief that while there might be occasional deviations, most individuals will remain true to their personality type throughout their lives.

Jung's treatment of the unconscious was less straightforward than his treatment of the conscious mind. Particularly, his idea of the collective unconscious set him apart from orthodox psychoanalytic thinking. He argued that human beings have inherited an instinctual apparatus that predisposes them to experience the world as their ancestors did. The numerous organizing principles of the collective unconscious are termed "archetypes." Examples include "the persona" — the face we present to the world; "the shadow" — the source of our animal instincts; and "the self" — the organizing principle by means of which we structure our personality.

Although the idea of the collective unconscious is the most distinctive part of Jung's approach, it is also the most problematic. Indeed, many people consider that it has more in common with mythology than scientific theory. A major problem is that the idea cannot easily be tested; consequently, any evidence that might count in its favor — for example, the similarity of many of the themes of myths — is necessarily circumstantial. There is also a problem with the idea that it is possible to recall ancestral experiences (though the extent to which this is suggested by Jung's theory is a matter of scholarly debate). Pretty much, the idea is a nonstarter; it would require the inheritance of acquired characteristics — what is sometimes called Lamarckism, after French biologist Jean-Baptiste de Lamarck — which is ruled out by the way that genes work (consider, for example, that the fact that your grandfather has learned to play the piano does not mean that you'll be born already able to play the piano).

Jung's oeuvre certainly constitutes an interesting variation on the theme of Freudian psychoanalysis. However, in the end, one must judge his work flawed for its lack of empirical warrant.

Collective unconscious: Jungian notion which refers to an unconscious, inherited part of the mind that is common to humanity as a whole. This idea, in conjunction with Jung's notion of archetypes, can be invoked in order to explain the universality of many of the stories, themes, and images which crop up in the mythologies of widely divergent cultures.

B. F. Skinner

B. F. Skinner, perhaps the twentieth century's most celebrated psychologist, was not in the least bit interested in what went on inside human minds. He believed that psychology should deal only with observable and measurable behavior; specifically, with the patterns of stimulus and response which underpin, or even constitute, behavior.

Born: 1904, Susquehanna, Pennsylvania
Importance: Foremost proponent of behaviorist psychology
Died: 1990, Cambridge, Massachusetts

The advantage of this radical behaviorism is that it puts psychology on a scientific footing; to the extent that its data are observable, it is, in principle, no different from any of the other sciences. Additionally, in focusing only on behavior, it sidesteps all the philosophical problems that are associated with the existence of an irreducible mental domain.

Skinner's most important substantive contribution to the science of psychology is his idea of "operant conditioning." This is best illustrated by means of an example. A rat runs around a maze, and comes across a lever. The rat might ignore the lever for a while, but at some point will press it, and will be rewarded with food. This has the effect of reinforcing the behavior which preceded the reward (the lever pushing). In this way, the rat is conditioned to press the lever. Thus, there is a "law of effect," first specified by psychologist Edward Thorndike, which holds that "responses to a situation which are followed by a rewarding state of affairs will be strengthened and become habitual responses to that situation."

The case described above is an instance of "positive reinforcement"; the lever-pushing is reinforced by the presentation of something the rat likes (i.e., food). Skinner also identified two other forms of conditioning; the first based on

Above: Skinner thought that all behavior is determined by various patterns of reinforcement. If a rat is rewarded with a snack for pressing a lever, then it will quickly learn to reproduce lever-pressing behavior.

"negative reinforcement," where a behavior is strengthened because it results in the removal of an aversive state of affairs (e.g., pain); the second based on "punishment," where a behavior is weakened because it results in the presentation of an aversive stimulus (e.g., pain).

It is important to understand just how radical Skinner's behaviorism actually is. He thought that almost all behavior is determined by the various patterns of reinforcement described above. Thus, the idea of free will is an illusion; human beings are in a strong sense the products of their environment. He was able to show the power of his ideas about behavior by conditioning a variety of animals to perform complex tasks; most famously, he taught pigeons to play table tennis.

However, although Skinner's ideas have been hugely influential, we now know that they are too simplistic. It turns out that what goes on inside the "black box" of the mind is tremendously important. Nevertheless, behaviorism remains an important approach in psychology, particularly in the psychotherapeutic field when combined with more sophisticated cognitive techniques.

Behaviorism

Wilhelm Wundt is perhaps the best candidate for the title of "founder" of the discipline of psychology. In 1879, he opened a laboratory at the University of Leipzig for the purpose of examining the functioning of the human mind. Wundt's approach to this task relied on *introspection*; experimental subjects were asked to analyze and report on their own conscious mental processes as they occurred under certain determinate conditions (for example, in response to a loud noise). The problem with this approach, however, was that it was impossible to verify the data that was accumulated; the researchers had no way of knowing that accurate reports were being given.

These kinds of worries led American John Watson to propose that psychology should focus entirely on observable behavior. The subject's mind would be strictly off limits to the psychologist. It was out of this thought that behaviorism was born.

The work of the great Russian physiologist Ivan Pavlov served as a model for what could be achieved in the discipline of behavioral psychology. He developed a theory of learning, now called classical conditioning, which made no reference to internal mental states, but emphasized instead the links between observable stimuli and responses.

Pavlov's groundbreaking insight, which he demonstrated with his famous dogs, was that it is possible to make use of an existing link between an unconditioned stimulus (e.g., food) and a response (e.g., salivation), in order to establish a link between a conditioned stimulus (e.g., a bell ringing) and the response (i.e., salivation). Thus, he found that if you repeat the process of ringing a bell at the same time as presenting food to a dog often enough, in the end you'll be able to elicit the kind of behavior the dog exhibits in the presence of food (i.e., salivation, excitement, etc.) merely by ringing the bell.

Watson demonstrated how this model could be extended to human learning (though not without violating modern ethical principles). He had noted that he could produce fear in a young child — little Albert — by striking a metal bar with a hammer just behind his head. Watson showed little Albert a rat at the same time as striking the metal bar. Little Albert's fear response quickly transferred to the rat — that is, the rat alone was soon enough to elicit a fear response from little Albert — and also to anything which reminded him of it (e.g., a rabbit, a dog, and cotton balls).

Classical conditioning, however, is limited as an explanation of human learning. It might explain a particular phobia, but it isn't going to explain how we are able to solve complex mathematical problems. It was partly these limitations which led B. F. Skinner to develop his theory of "operant conditioning." This showed how behaviors which had been spontaneously produced by organisms in their natural environments might be encouraged or discouraged by the patterns of "reinforcement" which were associated with them (thus, for example, rats can learn to run a maze if they are rewarded for each successful attempt).

The insights of behaviorism are still useful in the field of psychotheraphy, but its heyday has now passed; it turns out that we do need to take an interest in what goes on inside human minds. Nevertheless, in insisting on the importance of observation, measurement, and testability, behaviorism played an important part in getting psychology onto a scientific footing.

Abraham H. Maslow

Abraham H. Maslow was one of the most important figures in the humanistic psychology movement that emerged in the United States after World War II. In contrast to behaviorism and psychoanalysis, the humanistic approach, a "third force" in psychology, which owes much to existential philosophy, stresses the importance of human experience, the potential for personal growth, and the possibility of self-fulfilment.

Born: 1908, New York
Importance: Developed a psychological theory of self-actualization
Died: 1970, Menlo Park, California

It was Maslow's view that human motivation can be understood in terms of a hierarchy of needs, which ranges from basic physiological needs at the bottom, upward through safety needs, the need for belonging and love, and onward until at the top there is the need for "self-actualization," which refers to the possibility of realizing one's full potential, or "becoming everything that one is capable of becoming."

In the normal course of events, needs at the bottom of the hierarchy must be satisfied before needs at the higher levels will begin to exert a motivating force. Thus, for example, the starving person will not be concerned with their need for self-esteem, or their aesthetic needs, until their hunger has been satisfied. The higher up the hierarchy an individual progresses, the less their needs are related to biology, the more they are dependent upon their life experience, and the harder they are to satisfy.

Although everybody is capable of achieving self-actualization, Maslow argued that most people will not do so, or will do so only to a very limited degree. He mentioned as examples of people who have achieved their full potential: William James, Albert Einstein, Thomas Jefferson, Baruch Spinoza, and Abraham

Left: Maslow thought that human motivation could be understood in terms of a hierarchy of needs. More fundamental needs, such as the need for food, must be fulfilled before less pressing needs begin to exert a motivating force.

Lincoln. He argued that there are certain characteristics that are typical of self-actualizers: they tend to be, for example, spontaneous in action and thought; able to perceive reality accurately; relatively independent of their cultures; happy to tolerate uncertainty; creative; interested in problem solving; and capable of enjoying deep relationships with just a few people.

He also noted that self-actualizers seem to have many *peak experiences* in their lives; moments of extreme happiness and fulfilment, which often involve a loss of the sense of self, and which will frequently alter the future course of the person's behavior in a positive way. Maslow believed that everybody is capable of peak experiences, but self-actualizers have more of them than other people.

It isn't yet clear whether the kinds of ideas pioneered by Maslow have been wholly beneficial in helping people to achieve psychological health. However, humanistic psychology was certainly an important corrective to the scientism of behaviorist psychology and to the dogmatic reductionism of psychoanalysis.

The Enlightenment

The Enlightenment is the name given to an intellectual movement that began in England in the seventeenth century, and then developed primarily in France in the eighteenth. Its defining characteristic is that it championed the cause of reason in the face of the irrationality and superstition of much of the thought of this time. In Kant's words, the Enlightenment marked the "emergence of man from his self-imposed infancy."

This infancy consisted primarily of the subservience of man to the constraints of religious belief. All questions about the nature of the universe, human beings, and their place in the cosmos, were to be answered in terms of scriptural authority. The Church's power, in continental Europe at least, was overwhelming at this time; every aspect of a person's life was potentially the focus of its interest and anger. To fall foul of the requirement for religious orthodoxy was to run the risk of imprisonment, torture, and death.

It was in this context that thinkers such as John Toland and John Locke in England, and Voltaire and Denis Diderot in France, began to articulate the Enlightenment message. In its broadest terms, this held that human beings all have the ability to use reason in order to think, to act, to solve problems, to find out about the world, and to progress morally. It denied that authority, whether that of priests, sacred texts, or church tradition, could ever be a proper measure of truth. Enlightenment thinkers, therefore, tended to be atheists or deists, and they preached religious tolerance. Indeed, the idea of tolerance was central to the Enlightenment project. Voltaire, for example, in his *Treatise on Tolerance*, pleaded for "a universal tolerance" of all peoples and religions, on the grounds that "we should regard all men as our brothers."

The Enlightenment, of course, has been subjected to strong criticism. In particular, its critics allege that in sanctifying human reason, Enlightenment thinkers failed to recognize the significance of tradition, locality, and community. More radically, philosophers such as Nietzsche rejected altogether the idea that reason has a sovereign role to play in human affairs.

The Enlightenment project has also come under pressure from some of the more troubling aspects of modernity. The advent of globalization has brought into sharp focus the fact that not everybody is committed to the kinds of liberal values that are normally felt to underpin the Enlightenment. From the point of view of a radical Islamic cleric, for example, to suppose that Enlightenment values are universal values is just another example of Western imperialistic thinking.

> Let us all hope for the triumph of Light — of Right and Reason — for the victory of Fact over Falsehood, of Science over Superstition.
>
> Robert G. Ingersoll
> *The Journal*

Nevertheless, it would be hard to overstate the importance of the Enlightenment. It was, for example, a large part of the motivating force for the French revolution, which, although unsuccessful in its own terms, established the grounds for the emergence of ideas such as "the rights of man" into mainstream political culture. It also contributed to the intellectual context within which science flourished in the eighteenth and early nineteenth centuries. Above all else, though, the Enlightenment vision held out, and still holds out, the hope of a world united by the ability of human beings to reason.

Voltaire

Voltaire, born François-Marie Arouet, is the most significant of the Enlightenment thinkers. He spent a large part of his life advocating the cause of reason, and exposing the brutalities of religious authoritarianism. He was the enemy of ignorance, myth, and superstition and, more often than not, his target was Christianity.

Born: 1694, Paris, France
Importance: Championed the causes of reason in the face of religious intolerance
Died: 1778, Paris, France

Nevertheless, in his early years, he was committed to a sort of optimistic deism. He argued that the universe displayed the marks of divinity in the order and regularity which Newton had so brilliantly explicated; and he claimed that God had created humans with the kinds of moral dispositions necessary for them to live good lives.

Voltaire was always aware that this optimistic view was threatened by the presence of evil and suffering in the world. In his early writings, even if he was not able to deal adequately with the problem, he was able to deflect it, at least to his own satisfaction. However, as time went on, he began increasingly to move away from this position; most particularly, he became ever more critical of Gottfried Leibniz's philosophical optimism, which held, roughly speaking, that this world, created by a rational, perfect God, is the best of all possible worlds.

Voltaire's growing pessimism was reinforced by his experience of the senseless and arbitrary nature of much human misery. The Lisbon earthquake, in particular, seemed inexplicable in terms of an optimistic, providential deism. It occurred on All Saints' Day in 1755 when the churches were full; nine thousand buildings were destroyed, and thirty thousand people lost their lives. Voltaire's response, "Poem on the Lisbon Disaster," was a brilliant articulation of his new pessimism.

Unhappy mortals! Dark and mourning earth!
Affrighted gathering of human kind!
Eternal lingering of useless pain!
Come, ye philosophers, who cry, "All's well,"
And contemplate this ruin of a world.

His rejection of Leibnizian optimism found perhaps its most powerful expression in his satirical novel *Candide*. The eponymous hero lives in a senseless world characterized by arbitrary and unnecessary suffering. Yet Candide's mentor, Dr. Pangloss, in line with his "metaphysico-theologo-cosmolonigology," insists that all is for the best in the best of all possible worlds. As Candide moves from one disaster to another, he finds Pangloss's optimism increasingly implausible, and is brought to understand the absurdity of abstract philosophical speculation in the face of human suffering. The novel, however, ends on an positive note: despair is not the answer in the face of a heartless world; rather, one should engage in practical, efficacious action. As Candide puts it, "let us cultivate our garden."

Voltaire's greatness lies in the role that he played in the eventual triumph of the Enlightenment. The great American secularist Robert Green Ingersoll sums up Voltaire's life like this: "For half a century, past rack and stake, past dungeon and cathedral, past altar and throne, he carried with brave hands the sacred torch of Reason, whose light at last will flood the world."

> **Deism:** A belief in God that is based on reason rather than faith, revelation, or the authority of scripture. The rise of deism in the seventeenth century was linked to the view that it is possible to see the handiwork of a benevolent deity in the regularity and elegance of the workings of nature.

Jean-Jacques Rousseau

At the beginning of *The Social Contract*, his most important work, Jean-Jacques Rousseau claimed that "Man is born free; and everywhere he is in chains." This idea contains a neat reversal of what was the orthodox view of his age, namely, that in a state of nature, people's lives are nasty, short, and brutish; and that it is only through the influence of civilization that they have become otherwise.

Born: 1712, Geneva, Switzerland
Importance: Developed the idea of government by social contract
Died: 1778, Ermenonville, France

In rejecting this view, Rousseau committed himself instead to the idea that human beings were originally "noble savages," who lived a solitary, peaceful existence, concerned mainly with the satisfaction of their immediate needs, and having little use for foresight, language, or any of the other facets of a social existence.

It is not entirely obvious how Rousseau thought that savage man moved away from the state of nature. However, he was clear that once people began to enjoy fixed relations with each other, the conditions were ripe for the emergence of competitiveness, jealousy, and aggression; and that what really condemned people to lives of slavery was the emergence of private property.

Indeed, it was Rousseau's argument that civil society (roughly speaking, civilization) was effectively founded by the person who first enclosed and then claimed ownership over a piece of land. Once there were people who believed the claim, civil society, as a means of justifying and maintaining property relations — that is, relations of inequality — was inevitable. At root, then, private property lies at the heart of inequality and its associated moral depravity.

Rousseau did not think that it was possible for humankind to return to a state of nature, which left the problem of how humans are best to govern their affairs given present circumstances. This was the issue which he addressed in *The Social Contract*.

The argument he constructed in this work rests on the concept of "the general will." Outside of social groups, individuals are free to pursue their own specific, selfish interests. However, once people begin to live in fixed relations with other people, this kind of freedom is necessarily curtailed. Nevertheless, there is a way in which people may live in social groups, yet remain free; a social contract whereby each individual member of the group must form part of that group's sovereign body. Freedom then consists in acting in accordance with the "general will" of the group.

There are, of course, problems with this idea. Not least it requires that as members of the sovereign body, people set aside their own personal interests, and act only for the common good. If nothing else, the history of the twentieth century, with its terrifying examples of the horrors associated with certain kinds of "tyranny of the majority" — consider, for example, that both Hitler and Stalin would have won landslide victories had they held elections in their respective countries — teaches us that "the common good" isn't necessarily what motivates the political choices of mass publics. Nevertheless, in locating sovereignty in the will of the people, Rousseau's idea of the "general will" marked an important moment in the history of democratic thought, and secured his reputation as an important, if somewhat paradoxical, Enlightenment thinker.

Sovereign body: The sovereign body of a society is the locus of legitimate power. Thus, for example, according to Rousseau, in a society organized on the basis of the ideas found in his book *The Social Contract*, what might be called legislative government — that is, government which looks after the day-to-day running of society — derives its power and legitimacy from a sovereign body which embodies the general will of society.

Charles Darwin

Charles Darwin was responsible for probably the most powerful single idea in the history of science; namely, the idea of the evolution of species by the mechanism of natural selection.

Born: 1809, Shrewsbury, England
Importance: Discovered the theory of the evolution of species by natural selection
Died: 1882, Downe, England

Until the publication of his book *The Origin of the Species*, in 1859, which brought this idea to the world's attention, it was not possible to explain the complexity of the living world without making reference to a designer. The human eye, for example, simply seemed too complex, too highly wrought, to have emerged purely naturalistically. Darwin's importance is that he showed how this was wrong.

Darwin had read Thomas Malthus's famous essay on population, in which Malthus argued that the rate of growth of a population tends to outstrip its capacity to sustain itself. The lesson that Darwin derived from this is that the living world is through and through competitive. Every species tends to produce more individuals than can possibly survive, therefore, life is characterized by a struggle for existence; or, more precisely, by a struggle for reproduction. It is this insight that led to his theory of evolution by natural selection. The argument is as follows:

Within any given species there are variations in the inherited traits of its members. For example, some members might have sharp teeth, some might have blunt teeth. Variations which are helpful in the struggle for reproduction (for example, sharp teeth, if they help an individual to stay alive long enough to breed) will be passed on to offspring more often than variations which are not helpful (for example, blunt teeth, if they mean that an individual is unable to kill its prey). Therefore, over time, helpful variations will come to be predominant. So long as there are

Above: Thanks to the camouflage provided by industrial pollution in some 19th-century English cities, dark peppered moths survived longer than lighter-colored members of the same species. As a result, more dark specimens reproduced successfully, and soon came to dominate.

always new variations for natural selection to work upon, evolution will continue indefinitely.

This is an immensely powerful idea. It explains, for example, how the eye emerged without a designer; by means of tiny, incremental steps, each one beneficial in its own right.

In Darwin's day, the precise mechanism of inheritance, and the source of the variations upon which natural selection worked, was not known. It was only at the turn of the twentieth century, with the rediscovery of the work of Gregor Mendel, that this became clearer. One hundred years later, we now know that genes are the units of inheritance; and that, every so often, they mutate to produce new characteristics in an organism, which are then subject to Darwinian selection.

Darwin's importance cannot be overstated. He was the founder of modern evolutionary biology; the person who, in Julian Huxley's phrase, put the world of life into the domain of natural law.

Social Thought

Social Darwinism

Social Darwinism is based on the claim that it is possible to make use of Darwinian concepts in order to understand society and the relationships which people have with each other. According to social Darwinists, societies progress because people aggressively pursue their own self-interest in competition with other people doing the same thing. They are competing primarily for economic success, and the "fittest," those people most adapted to the demands of competition, deservedly rise to the top. If a person is not successful, it indicates a lack of "fitness," and, by extension, that they are not deserving of the rewards that fitness brings.

The nineteenth-century social theorist Herbert Spencer is probably the best known exponent of social Darwinist ideas. In his view, social Darwinism translated naturally into a celebration of the individualistic, competitive ethos of laissez-faire capitalism. Spencer thought it quite natural that there were economic winners and losers under capitalism. He opposed social reform and government intervention to help those disadvantaged by the system, on the grounds that there should be no interference in what was a natural mechanism for sorting out the fit from the unfit. Thus, in *The Study of Sociology* he argued that if "the unworthy are helped to increase, by shielding them from that mortality which their unworthiness would naturally entail, the effect is to produce, generation after generation, a greater unworthiness."

Spencer's ideas were enthusiastically adopted by many capitalists at the end of the nineteenth century, particularly in the United States, as a means to justify their wealth and resist the call for social reform. However, his kind of crude social Darwinism was relatively short-lived. Even by the first decade of the twentieth century, Spencer's ideas were beginning to fall into disrepute. Nevertheless, social Darwinism remains a factor in the way in which people think about evolutionary ideas; only now, it is as a source of suspicion, rather than a copper-bottomed, biologically informed political philosophy.

There is a tendency to suppose that social Darwinism had little to do with Charles Darwin himself. This is not quite right. Even Darwin flirted with this kind of thinking. Particularly, he worried about the social consequences of the fact that it is possible for human beings to protect themselves against the demands of natural selection. Thus in *The Descent of Man* he noted that:

> We build asylums for the imbecile, the maimed and the sick; we institute poor-laws; and our medical men exert their utmost skill to save the life of everyone to the last moment...Thus the weak members of civilized societies propagate their kind. No one who has attended to the breeding of domestic animals will doubt that this must be highly injurious to the race of man.

Darwin, of course, was a product of his time, so we mustn't judge him too harshly for this kind of thinking. And thankfully, his idea of evolution by natural selection is powerful enough to transcend the kind of social and political baggage that even he on occasion was tempted to attach to it.

Laissez-faire capitalism: Capitalism is an economic system based on the private ownership of the means of production, which sees individuals and companies, motivated by profit, compete with each other in order to sell products in a free market. Capitalism is based on laissez-faire principles if there is no government interference in this process, even if its consequences involve social deprivation.

Max Weber

Max Weber is arguably the twentieth century's most important sociologist. He conceived of sociology as the scientific, objective study of social action. Perhaps the most distinctive feature of his approach is that he insisted that in order to understand the actions of human beings it is necessary to understand the meanings which they attach to them.

Born: 1861, Erfurt, Prussia (now Germany)

Importance: A founding father of sociology, he showed how ideas and ideology can drive social change

Died: 1920, Munich, Germany

It was Weber's claim that no matter how accurately we are able to predict a typical course of action, if we don't correctly apprehend the motives which underlie it, then we have only uncovered meaningless statistical probability; in Weber's terms, our explanation lacks "adequacy at the level of meaning."

It might be thought that the point which Weber is making here is obvious; clearly, if we want to understand social action, then we've got to understand what motivates it. However, one might concede this point, yet still insist that it is possible to analyze society in a way that does not require the interpretative understanding of social action. For example, Karl Marx argued that social change is driven by contradictions in the economic systems of societies; arguably, this kind of large-scale social change has nothing to do with the meanings which individuals attach to their actions. Weber, however, disagreed; and in perhaps his most famous work, *The Protestant Ethic and the Spirit of Capitalism*, he showed that even something as significant as the transition from feudalism to capitalism can be driven by ideas and meanings.

Weber noticed that there were statistical correlations between the emergence of nascent forms of capitalism in Germany and the prevalence of Calvinistic Protestantism. He argued that this is explained because Calvinism is a theology of predestination. The followers believed that whether or not they were going to heaven was predetermined; there was nothing that they could do to affect their destiny. Such a belief carries with it a terrible burden; a constant fear of the possibility of hellfire. But there was a kind of psychological trick that helped to lessen the anxiety. Worldly success was thought to be an excellent indication of an individual having found God's favor. Therefore, if they worked hard and abstained from enjoying the fruits of their labors, then although their successes wouldn't affect their destiny, they would surely be a *sign* that they were among the chosen. The result of this was the development of conditions ripe for capitalism.

> Sociology ... is a science concerning itself with the interpretive understanding of social action and thereby with a causal explanation of its course and consequences.
>
> Max Weber *Economy and Society*

Weber was well aware that this was not the whole story of the emergence of capitalism. However, his analysis provided a corrective to those theories which sought to explain social phenomena in purely material terms. Thus, Weber was able to show how an understanding of social action at the level of meaning can be central to a full understanding of social processes.

Weber's influence remains strong to this day. Indeed, in a world characterized by the reemergence of religious fundamentalism and nationalism, Weber's insistence that social explanation is about ideas and meanings as well as economics and social structure seems highly prescient. Social actors have inner lives; if we want to understand how they act, it is necessary to understand the stories they tell themselves about their actions.

Social Thought

Sociology

Sociology is the systematic, scientific study of the development, structure, and functioning of social groups and society. People have always been interested in how society functions. Plato, for example, in *The Republic*, attempted to specify the organization of the perfect society. However, it wasn't until the nineteenth century with the work of Auguste Comte, and then Herbert Spencer, that sociology emerged as a distinct academic discipline.

Right from the start, there has been no general agreement within the discipline as to how it should best go about the task of analyzing society (which presumably motivated Henri Poincaré's remark that "sociology is the science with the greatest number of methods and the least results"). Thus, for example, at the end of the nineteenth century, Emile Durkheim urged that social facts — for instance, the rate of suicide — should be treated as if they were things, subject to the influence of other social facts (in the case of suicide, the level of social integration). Durkheim conceived of sociology as a positivistic science; it should aim to track the law-like relationships between the measurable aspects of society. Max Weber, in contrast, insisted that sociology had to be about more than this; it had also to look at the meanings that individuals attach to their actions. In other words, sociology must pursue the interpretative understanding of social action.

This lack of agreement among sociologists has led some people to suppose that sociology is not a real science. Somewhat ironically, many sociologists would agree, but deny that it is a problem. Indeed, some go so far as to suggest that human behavior is in principle beyond the reach of the scientific method; for example, that what appear to be regular patterns of social behavior are in fact a by-product of the way in which individuals interpret, understand, organize, and respond to the flux of social experience.

There is perhaps one thing that is common to most sociological approaches; they tend to manifest a commitment to what Leda Cosmides and John Tooby have called the Standard Social Science Model. This holds that the mind has no specific content; it is simply a general purpose machine suited for tasks such as learning and reasoning. Therefore, whatever is found in human minds has come in from the outside; from the environment and the social world.

The consequences of this commitment are far reaching in terms of the kinds of explanations that count as properly sociological. For example, almost all students of sociology will have been taught that biology plays little or no role in determining human behavior. If there is conflict in society, for instance, then it is *not* to be explained in terms of categories that refer to an innate predisposition toward aggression. Rather, it is to be seen as a function of a disruption in society's normative system; or the result of a fundamental conflict of interest between opposing social groups.

However, with the emergence of evolutionary psychology, even this commitment to the Standard Social Science Model is coming under threat. Indeed, more than this, the discipline of sociology itself is under threat. As our understanding of the mind increases, the room for distinctively sociological explanations of human behavior grows smaller. Thus, it is not absolutely beyond the realms of possibility that by the end of the twenty-first century, sociology will be just another sub-discipline of neuroscience.

Mahatma Gandhi

Mohandas (Mahatma) Gandhi was one of the most admired and influential people of the twentieth century. In showing that it was possible to achieve significant political change by passive, nonviolent protest, he inspired a generation of political leaders, including Martin Luther King, Albert Lithuli, and Helder Camara. Upon his assassination in 1948, Jawaharlal Nehru, a future prime minister of India, was led to declare that "the light has gone out of our lives and there is darkness everywhere."

Born: 1869, Porbandar, India
Importance: Showed how a philosophy of nonviolence could work politically
Died: 1948, Delhi, India

Gandhi's philosophy of nonviolence (*ahimsa*) was based partly on his belief that all human beings have souls, no matter how reprehensible their actions. This means that there is always the possibility of appealing to their humanity, or fellow-feeling, in order to persuade them to change their views or behavior. Therefore, almost without exception, violence is unnecessary.

Moreover, violence has effects that are either permanent, or very hard to reverse. Consequently, for it to be justified, one would need to be absolutely certain of the justice of the position motivating the violence, and also that it would have the desired outcome. However, since human beings are fallible, such a certainty is never available, thus ruling out violence as an appropriate course of action.

Gandhi was fully aware that people are sometimes led to violence by the desperation of the situations which confront them. Thus, for example, one might think that the Americans were right to drop the atomic bomb on Hiroshima, because it hastened the end of the war in the Pacific, and thereby saved lives. However, it was Gandhi's view that it isn't possible to separate means from

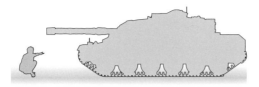

Above: Gandhi's philosophy of "ahimsa" held that almost without exception, violence is unnecessary. Even when confronted by the violence of our oppressor we should respond nonviolently, in order to open their hearts in the face of our suffering.

ends in this fashion. If one uses dubious means to attain good ends, inevitably those ends will be compromised and distorted by the immorality which brought them about.

If violence, then, is not the way to solve disputes, or to end great injustices, what will take its place? Gandhi's extraordinary answer is that one should seek to awaken the essential humanity of an adversary through one's own suffering:

> … if you want something really important to be done you must not merely satisfy the reason, you must move the heart also. The appeal of reason is more to the head but the penetration of the heart comes from suffering. It opens up the inner understanding in man. Suffering is the badge of the human race, not the sword.

This idea underpinned his commitment to nonviolent, political protest. Many people will suspect that its utility is limited to very particular circumstances. Nevertheless, if these circumstances obtain, it can be a very powerful mechanism for social and political change, as his own example in India, and that of Martin Luther King in the United States, showed.

Social Thought

Theodor Adorno

The rise of fascism and the horrors of the Holocaust cast a long shadow over the work of Theodor Adorno. Although he accepted Marx's analysis of capitalism, he was confronted with the stark reality that modern capitalist societies appeared not to be producing progressive political movements. Indeed, quite the opposite; in Nazi Germany, for example, the working class had been coopted to the cause of fascism, which led ultimately to the depravities of the gas chambers.

Born: 1903, Frankfurt am Main, Germany
Importance: Showed how Enlightenment reason might be associated with the rise of fascism
Died: 1969, Visp, Switzerland

In *Dialectic of Enlightenment*, a difficult work which he wrote with Frankfurt school colleague Max Horkheimer, Adorno argued that the crisis in modernity is linked to the dominance of a certain kind of reason. Enlightenment thinking, based upon a fear of the unknown, had produced a totalizing, instrumental rationality, which sought to incorporate everything in its path. Thus, human beings, subject to a process of reification, had become objects to be dominated in the name of social and political control. National Socialism, then, was the outcome of a technocratic rationality that had effectively dehumanized people.

Part of what made the rise of fascism so troubling for thinkers inclined toward Marxism was that it demonstrated that huge swaths of people were prepared to tolerate activities which in other ages would have been considered barbarous. This led Adorno to wonder whether there was a personality syndrome that might explain the patterns of obedience and complicity which characterized the Nazi era. The culmination of these thoughts was the publication of *The Authoritarian Personality*, written in collaboration with a group of Berkeley researchers.

In this work, Adorno argued that authoritarianism was a particular cognitive style (roughly speaking, a way of thinking), and that an individual's social, political, and economic views formed an integrated pattern which reflected underlying tendencies in their personality. He found that individuals holding anti-Semitic attitudes tended also to be prejudiced against other minority groups, for example, blacks and homosexuals; in other words, there appeared to be a general predisposition toward prejudice. Adorno suggested that prejudice is associated with a particular constellation of beliefs and attitudes which are characteristic of authoritarian personalities; in particular, authoritarians will tend to have rigid beliefs; hold "conventional" values; be intolerant of weakness and ambiguity in themselves and others; be punitive; and be highly respectful of authority.

Adorno, and his fellow authors, even went so far as to construct an "F Scale" in order to measure implicit authoritarian attitudes. In their research they found that authoritarianism was strongly linked with both anti-Semitism and ethnocentrism, suggesting that authoritarians might be predisposed to accept anti-democratic ideologies such as fascism.

There is no doubt that there are flaws in Adorno's authoritarian personality study. Nevertheless, fifty years on, it remains a significant and important work.

Social Thought

Michel Foucault

Michel Foucault was no ordinary philosopher. His range of influences extended well beyond the standard philosophical canon; indeed, although Nietzsche was a great inspiration, Foucault's work perhaps has more in common with history and sociology than it does with philosophy. Nevertheless, he retains his significance as a philosopher for the original and striking way that he rethought the relationship between power and knowledge.

Born: 1926, Poitiers, France
Importance: Showed that power and knowledge are integrally related
Died: 1984, Paris, France

It was Foucault's claim that human beings are constituted as knowing, knowable, and self-knowing subjects in relations of power and discourse. By this he meant, roughly speaking, that our knowledge of other people and of ourselves is a function of particular ways of looking at the world. Thus, for example, in terms of the discourses of modern psychiatry, people with schizophrenia are mentally "ill"; they have a "condition" that is specifiable in terms of more or less precise diagnostic criteria; and they are subject to particular medical interventions in order to treat and control their illness.

According to Foucault, power and knowledge are integrally related. Thus, for example, in *Madness and Civilization*, he showed how the "dividing practices" that separate people into the categories "sane" and "insane" function as a form of social control; to label a person as mentally ill is to neutralize the threat that is posed to the social order by their *otherness*.

The most effective forms of social control are those that are self-imposed. Thus, for instance, if it is possible to control the attitudes which people hold toward their own sexuality, then "deviant" sexual behaviors need never become visible in society: individuals will police themselves.

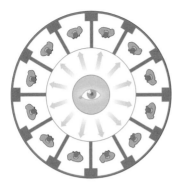

Left: Foucault argued that the panopticon — a circular prison with cells arranged around a central observation post — is the consummate disciplinary technology. Prisoners must constantly monitor their own behavior, under ever-present fear of being watched.

In his book *Discipline and Punish*, Foucault showed how Jeremy Bentham's idea of the panopticon — a kind of prison — was based upon eliciting the self-imposed discipline of the prisoners it housed. The structure of the panopticon means that it functions effectively whether or not prison guards are actually present. Prisoners do not know whether they are being watched so they must act as if surveillance were constant and unending. In effect, then, prisoners become their own prison guards.

According to Foucault, the panopticon, as an integrated, disciplinary technology, binds together power, knowledge, and the control of bodies and space. It is possible to see an equivalence here with wider society: social control is most effective when individuals police themselves in terms of the discourses and practices of sexual, moral, physical, and psychological normality.

If power is all-pervasive, as Foucault suggested, then it isn't clear that people can ever free themselves from its effects. However, the value of philosophy is that it helps us to understand the power structures that underpin the various forms of social control. In this sense, then, philosophy is the first step on the path toward resistance.

Peter Singer

Peter Singer is perhaps the most controversial philosopher living today. His most vociferous critics have suggested — entirely erroneously — that he is some kind of Nazi; in Germany, his lectures have been disrupted, while in the United States, his appointment as Professor of Bioethics at Princeton attracted fierce criticism. The source of such strong feelings are the views that he holds about topics such as euthanasia, abortion, and animal rights.

Born: 1946, Melbourne, Australia
Importance: The leading moral philosopher of the latter part of the twentieth century
Died:

Singer is a consequentialist about ethics; this means that he thinks that the rightness of an action should be judged in terms of its outcomes. Specifically, it is his view that we should strive to maximize the satisfaction of preferences. In other words, an action is right to the extent that it increases the ability of any beings affected by the action to satisfy the preferences which they hold (perhaps, for example, a preference for material comfort or for academic achievement). Although this formulation might seen unproblematic, when one thinks about it closely, it quickly leads to difficulties.

Consider the case of non-human animals. In his book *Animal Liberation*, Singer argues that it is wrong to treat humans and animals differently simply because they are different species. Rather, what counts is whether they have the kinds of lives which are worth living. Part of what is important here is the extent to which they have, or are likely again to have, preferences at all (which might, for example, be rooted in their plans for the future, a sense of their own well-being, attachments to others, and so on).

It is now possible to see how interesting ethical dilemmas might arise. For example, should one rescue a human being who

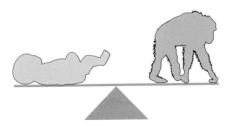

Left: Singer's ethical views are controversial. In some circumstances, he argues, the life of a great ape might be more valuable than the life of a newborn baby.

is in a persistent vegetative state if it means sacrificing the life of a great ape? Singer's position, consistently applied, will normally require that the great ape is saved; in this situation, the human being simply does not have the kind of life that justifies allowing the great ape to die.

It is possible to extend this kind of analysis into different areas. For example, if a baby is born with severe brain damage, it isn't obvious that euthanasia will always be wrong. The newborn infant

> The notion that human life is sacred just because it is human life is medieval.
>
> Peter Singer *Independent on Sunday*

will likely have only a severely restricted sense of self; it will have no conscious attachments to other people, no plans for the future, no cognitive investment in its own survival, and, potentially, only suffering and misery in the rest of its life. In these kinds of circumstances, it is Singer's belief that it can be right, with the parents' consent, to take active steps to end the life of the infant.

This makes it easy to see how Singer's views get him into trouble. Yet, for all that, it isn't obvious where he goes wrong in his arguments. Perhaps the moral of the story, then, is that philosophy can sometimes lead one to uncomfortable conclusions.

Niccolò Machiavelli

Niccolò Machiavelli famously claimed that successful political leaders need to possess the strength of a lion and the cunning of a fox. This was a lesson he first learned when, as a Florentine diplomat, he was able to observe firsthand some of the most celebrated political figures of his age in action. In *The Prince*, his now notorious essay on the art of leadership, he cites with approval the ruthless cunning that Cesare Borgia employed to dispose of his political rivals. It was Machiavelli's view that leaders had to learn how *not* to be good in order to rule effectively.

Born: 1469, Florence
Importance: Showed that the art of politics depends on flexibility and strength in the face of real circumstances
Died: 1527, Florence

In this sense, Machiavelli was an amoralist. He thought that rulers should set aside moral considerations when making political decisions; their only concern should be with retaining their grip on power. This meant that it was inevitable that leaders would sometimes have to be cruel, have to rule by dread of punishment, and have to behave in ways that would be judged to be immoral by commonly accepted standards.

However, it would be a mistake to think that Machiavelli favored nefarious behavior for its own sake; his political thinking was a lot more sophisticated than that. The highest calling of a leader, or, to use Machiavelli's terminology, a prince, is to strive for honor and glory. It is a mark of the *virtú* of a prince that he is willing to do whatever is necessary in the face of unpredictable fortune to achieve this end. However, this does not justify cruelty for cruelty's sake. Thus, Machiavelli argued that:

> Well used are those cruelties ... that are carried out in a single stroke, done out of necessity to protect oneself,

and are not continued but are instead converted into the greatest possible benefits for the subjects. Badly used are those cruelties which, although being few at the outset, grow with the passing time instead of disappearing. Those who follow the first method can remedy their condition with God and with men ... the others cannot possibly survive.

There is a related point here. Machiavelli believed that effective leadership, even though it required that rulers occasionally put aside moral considerations, would tend to have good outcomes for all. Thus, for example, he argued that the excessively merciful prince, by tolerating disorder, will often bring greater harm to a community than the cruel prince who creates harmony through fear. Likewise, generosity in a leader will almost always lead to discontent; in the end, the prince who is predisposed to outlandish displays of spending will have to tax the people in order to pay for such excessses, and will be resented and disliked as a result.

Machiavelli, then, is a much more sophisticated thinker than is often thought. His originality lies in his desire to confront the grubby realities of political life. By insisting that the mark of great leadership is the ability to master the demands of unpredictable fortune, he showed himself to be the first truly modern political theorist.

Amoralism: To behave amorally is to behave in such a way which takes no account of moral judgments. It is not to be immoral, since this would be to accept the relevance of moral claims, but rather to reject the appropriateness or possibility of moral judgment altogether.

Adam Smith

Although Adam Smith's reputation rests primarily on his authorship of *The Wealth of Nations*, perhaps the most important treatise of political economy ever written, the proper entry point into his work is his earlier essay on moral philosophy, *Theory of Moral Sentiments*.

Born: 1723, Kirkcaldy, Scotland
Importance: Articulated the definitive theory of laissez-faire economics
Died: 1790, Edinburgh, Scotland

In this work, he argued that human beings are endowed with both instinct and reason. The instincts, concerning the need for self-preservation and the propagation of the species, are the wellspring of human action. Thus, Smith wrote, for example, of "hunger, thirst, the passion which unites the two sexes, the love of pleasure, and the dread of pain."

The question then is, given the power of the instincts, how are people to form moral judgments; to hold even their own behavior to account, and sometimes to conclude that they have themselves behaved badly?

Smith's answer, roughly speaking, was that we have a capacity for sympathy, which enables us to imagine ourselves in the position of other people, and thereby to look back at our own behavior. Thus, we internalize a kind of impartial spectator, allowing us to judge both our own behavior and the behavior of others. It is by a process of mutual sympathy and accommodation between individuals that the social and moral order emerges.

It is not clear how well this conception fits with the position Smith adopted in *The Wealth of Nations*. Certainly the idea that humans are driven by instincts of self-preservation and self-interest remained constant between the two books. However, in *The Wealth of Nations*, he argued that the social and moral order is an *unintended* consequence of the pursuit of self-interest; in a free market, a system of perfect liberty, individuals acting in their own self-interest will be led by an "invisible hand" to benefit society as a whole.

To get a sense of this argument, imagine setting up a shop selling philosophy books. By doing so, you meet a demand (for books) and create employment. Rational self-interest means that you'll price your books at the right level — otherwise people will buy them from your competitors; and you'll pay your workers appropriate wages — otherwise they'll work elsewhere. And if you decide only to sell books by English philosophers, then your competitors, acting rationally to maximize their profits, will exploit the selling opportunities available in continental philosophy.

> It is not from the benevolence of the butcher, the brewer, or the baker, that we expect our dinner, but from their regard to their own interest.
>
> Adam Smith *The Wealth of Nations*

Thus, one can see, in theory at least, how self-interest, together with our ability to respond rationally to the market, leads to the emergence of a stable and mutually beneficial economic system. The key phrase, though, is "in theory," for laissez-faire economics has never worked out quite this way. This has hit Smith's reputation. His name, perhaps unfairly, is just as often associated with the excesses of Victorian capitalism, as it is with the liberalism which informed his philosophical, political, and economic thinking.

Libertarianism

The central claim of a libertarian philosophy is that the State has no role to play in the conduct of the lives of individuals. Thus, for example, libertarians will argue that things such as sexual behavior, gun ownership, and drug use should not be subject to restrictions imposed by society. The only exception to this general principle is the role that a minimal State must play in ensuring that the freedoms of individuals are not violated.

It is possible to get a sense of the radicalism of the libertarian view by considering the kinds of things which it rules out. For example, almost all libertarians will reject the idea that the State should provide a "safety net," via a welfare system, to protect people who for various reasons are in need. Libertarians hold that such a system violates the rights of individuals by coercing them to contribute to it. In addition, it encourages the emergence of a "dependency culture," which sees people choosing state benefits rather than work. Thus, a welfare system is not only immoral, it is counterproductive.

Libertarians also oppose any attempt on the part of the State to pursue the goal of greater "social justice" via a taxation system that takes a greater proportion of the income of higher earners than it does of lower earners. Again, it is possible to pitch this opposition in moral terms, by claiming that it violates the principle that individuals should be equal before the law.

To the extent that libertarians deny that the State has a role to play in combating the extremes of inequality, it raises the issue of what to do about poverty. The problem for the libertarian account is that it is at least arguable that poverty deprives people of their ability to make choices. Thus, if a society organized on libertarian principles results in greater poverty than there would be otherwise, it might have the effect of reducing the total amount of liberty.

There are, however, a number of responses that a libertarian can make to this argument. For example, she can deny that libertarianism will be associated with poverty; following thinkers like Adam Smith and F. A. Hayek, many libertarians think that a society organized on laissez-faire principles will be more efficient, and therefore more generally prosperous, than societies based on other economic arrangements. Or they can argue that while poverty might affect the ability of people to do things, it doesn't affect their liberty, since liberty means merely having those choices available which are guaranteed by individual rights.

> Liberty not only means that the individual has both the opportunity and burden of choice; it also means that he must bear the consequences of his actions…Liberty and responsibility are inseparable.
>
> F. A. Hayek *The Constitution of Liberty*

Libertarianism is in many ways an attractive philosophy. But there is something *Alice in Wonderland* about it. In particular, the kinds of political upheavals that would be required for society to be organized on libertarian principles are not going to happen, at least in the foreseeable future; and, as in the case of Marxism, it's a sure bet that libertarianism in practice would be very different from libertarianism in theory.

Edmund Burke

Edmund Burke was not a systematic philosopher. Rather, like his contemporary Thomas Paine, he was a political thinker who sought to influence the course of social and political events through his writing. Unlike Paine, though, he was politically conservative, a staunch defender of the virtues of prejudice and tradition in the face of a radical politics that sought revolutionary change based on abstract notions of universal rights and democratic government.

Born: 1729, Dublin, Ireland
Importance: Author of the standard conservative defense of tradition, and organic, rather than revolutionary, social change
Died: 1797, Beaconsfield, England

Burke's conservatism was rooted in a deep suspicion of radical politics based upon untested, abstract principles. It was his belief that it is always a mistake to destroy political and social arrangements which are rooted in the long history of a society. A state takes the form that it does because it has in important respects served the citizens it represents. It is not prudent, then, to bring down in one fell swoop what has been bequeathed to the present by antiquity.

Burke articulated this view most famously in his book, *Reflections on the French Revolution*, in which he sought to persuade the British authorities that the dangers of the revolution justified an armed intervention. He contrasted the French revolution with the "Glorious Revolution" of 1688, where William of Orange marched on London unopposed to replace the Catholic James II. The latter was about righting the corruption of the state, without destroying the tradition upon which it was based. The French revolution, in contrast, sought to throw off the past in its entirety. It was an attempt at a root-and-branch reconstruction of society on the basis of a philosophy of universal rights that had been tested only in the court of abstract reason.

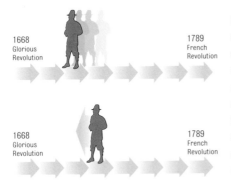

1668
Glorious
Revolution

1789
French
Revolution

1668
Glorious
Revolution

1789
French
Revolution

Left: Edmund Burke thought that politics should be rooted in an understanding of the significance of tradition and inherited values. Political thinkers must look backward to the past, as well as forward into the future.

There was no recognition of tradition and inherited values. It was, Burke thought, bound to fail.

It is important to recognize that Burke was not an unsophisticated thinker. His conservatism was informed by the belief that it is necessary to pay attention to history and circumstance. Thus, for example, the position he took on the events leading up to the American revolution was much more nuanced than might be expected. He rejected the idea that Britain should adopt an aggressive stance toward their rebellious colonists. Rather, in a celebrated parliamentary speech, he urged that Britain should make concessions in order to secure the loyalty of America. History and experience suggested that force wouldn't work, so whatever might be felt about the right of Britain to levy unpopular taxes, for example, the only prudent course of action was conciliation.

Burke's ideas have informed the thoughts of successive generations of political theorists. His arguments against the French revolution now seem a little shrill; but the ideas which motivated them retain their significance, and form part of the armory of many a conservative thinker.

Political Thought

Thomas Paine

Thomas Paine lived in an era that witnessed two great political convulsions: the American and French revolutions. It is a testament to his importance as a radical, political thinker and propagandist that he played a role in both.

Born: 1737, Thetford, England
Importance: Early advocate of the idea that all people are born equal
Died: 1809, New York

He first came to prominence in 1776 with the publication of "Common Sense," an essay he wrote while working as the editor of the *Philadelphia Magazine*. Inspired by the initial skirmishes of the American Revolutionary War, he argued that it was both a moral duty and a practical necessity for America to seek its independence from Britain. The alternative was to see America subjugated by their foreign ruler.

"Common Sense" was an immediate success. Not only did it sell in huge numbers, it also reached the eyes of some of the major figures of the American Revolution, thus securing Paine's reputation. Indeed, George Washington famously had Paine read aloud to his troops before the battle of Trenton:

These are the times that try men's souls. The summer soldier and the sunshine patriot will, in this crisis, shrink from the service of his country; but he that stands it now, deserves the love and thanks of man and woman.

After the Revolutionary War, Paine returned to his native England, where he wrote *The Rights of Man*, a defense of the principles of the French Revolution. In it, he argued that all people are born with equal, natural rights. However, it is inevitable that humans beings living in groups will occasionally come to conflict and disagreement, and that rights will be violated. Consequently, in order to secure the rights of everybody, people entrust those rights which they cannot uphold individually — for example, the right to redress for a harm — into the care of government. The only legitimate government, then, is one which is established by the people as a whole; a government of the people, and for the people. According to Paine, the kind of government which most successfully fulfils this role is democratic republicanism.

The Rights of Man marked something of a turning point in Paine's life. The furious reaction it provoked in Britain forced him to flee to France, where he initially met with good fortune, gaining a seat at the National Convention. Quite quickly, however, he fell foul of Robespierre and was imprisoned, and only released after the intervention of the American statesman James Monroe. He carried on writing, but his later books *The Age of Reason* and *Agrarian Justice*, despite their considerable merits, did not have the popular appeal of his earlier works.

Paine remains a celebrated figure in the history of the political left. He was not a brilliantly original thinker, but he was a brilliantly effective writer, and he is still able to move people by the power of his prose.

> One of the strongest natural proofs of the folly of hereditary right in kings is that nature disproves it, otherwise she would not so frequently turn it into ridicule by giving mankind an ass for a lion.
>
> Thomas Paine
> *Common Sense*

Jeremy Bentham

Although Jeremy Bentham died nearly 200 years ago, it is still possible to catch a glimpse of him if you're passing through the cloisters at University College, London; for there, inside a glass box, sitting on a chair, are his remains, stuffed for posterity.

No doubt this sounds a little bizarre, but it was Bentham's hope that this "auto-icon," as it is called, would keep his ideas alive amongst his followers.

Born: 1748, London, England
Importance: Popularized a system of ethics called utilitarianism
Died: 1832, London, England

The idea for which Bentham is best known is the ethical doctrine called utilitarianism, which rests on what is commonly termed the Greatest Happiness Principle. This holds that one should approve or disapprove of an action, "according to the tendency which it appears to have to augment or diminish the happiness of the party whose interest is in question ... I say that of every action whatsoever; and therefore not only of every action of a private individual, but of every measure of government."

Of course, the immediate question which this raises is how is it possible to judge whether an action is likely to promote happiness or not. Somewhat surprisingly, it was Bentham's view that it was possible to employ a "felicific calculus" to make precise calculations in this regard. Specifically, he argued that it was possible to quantify happiness in terms of such qualities as intensity, duration, and purity. Thus, an action is right if, after adding up all the pleasures on one side and all the pains on the other, the balance comes down on the side of happiness.

Utilitarianism remains hugely influential to this day (albeit in guises far more sophisticated than Bentham's). Nevertheless, it does suffer from a number of significant flaws. For a start, there is something a little cold and inflexible about the ethical principle

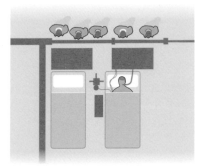

which underpins it. Consider, for example, Bentham's famous
prison design, the "panopticon." This was built so that prisoners
would never know whether they were being watched by a guard,
although it was possible that they were being watched all the
time. As a result, they had to monitor their own behavior.
A perfect utilitarian design — prisoners are controlled, but do
not suffer unnecessarily — but strangely inhuman nevertheless.

The other major difficulty associated with Bentham's version
of utilitarianism is that it seems to require that in certain
circumstances we sacrifice the right of a particular individual to
enjoy happiness in order to promote the greatest happiness of the
greatest number. For example, supposing that by punishing an
innocent person, we can, because of the deterrent effect, save the
lives of hundreds of people. It seems at least possible that in terms
of Bentham's utilitarianism this would be the right thing to do.

Although Bentham was not a truly great philosopher, his name
is associated with a philosophical theory which still has legs some
two hundred years after his death. This is not something which all
great philosophers can claim. Bentham's legacy, then, is secure.

Karl Marx

In terms of the impact of his ideas, Karl Marx is the most significant of the modern philosophers. The socialist revolutions in Russia and China were inspired by his writings, and legions of people around the world still call themselves Marxists.

Born: 1818, Trier, Prussia (now Germany)
Importance: Developed what is now called "Marxism," a theory of historical, revolutionary change
Died: 1883, London, England

Marx's view was that it is in the nature of human beings to cooperate together in a process of collective, freely chosen labor. It is in this way that people achieve proper self-realization. But Marx identified a problem: in all hitherto existing societies this process has been distorted by the existence of social classes; by the division between those who own and control the productive process and those who do not. The central idea here is that there have always been large groups of people who are alienated from the labor process; they have no control over the circumstances in which they engage in productive activity and no control over the products of their labor. As a result, they are alienated from their own essential nature.

It is in capitalist societies that this kind of alienation reaches its apex. Capitalism is characterized by a fundamental conflict between two great classes, the bourgeoisie — the owners of the means of production (such as factories) — and the proletariat, who own only their own labor power. The proletariat are alienated because they are forced to sell their labor under circumstances not of their own choosing; their productive energies are expended for the benefit of the class that exploits them. Marx described the proletarian's experience of alienation like this:

> … he does not fulfil himself in his work but denies
> himself, has a feeling of misery rather than well-being,

does not develop freely his mental and physical energies but is physically exhausted and mentally debased. The worker, therefore, feels himself at home only during his leisure time, whereas at work he feels homeless.

However, all is not lost for the proletariat, for it was Marx's view that they are the bearers of the emancipatory potential of humankind. Capitalism is riddled with contradictions, which in the end will result in its downfall; and it is the proletariat who will bring this about. As a class-for-itself, a class aware of its own reality and situation, it is the destiny of the proletariat to abolish all class distinctions, instituting a new form of society — communism — based on collective ownership. In doing so, the proletariat will end the alienation of people from the products of their labor, from the labor process itself, and from their essential humanity.

Marx's view of social change from natural communism

Through history, the division between owners and non-owners has been at the root of social conflict.

Primitive Communism: Hunter-gathering lifestyle; very simple technology and common ownership.

Ancient: Social order founded on the division between owners and slaves

Feudal: Mode of production based on agriculture. Landowning lords and bonded serfs.

Capitalist: Industrial mode of production characterized by the division between the bourgeoisie and proletariat.

Political Thought

F. A. Hayek

After World War II, there was a widely held view in Europe — the western part of it, at any rate — that economies functioned best on the basis of a mixture of state and private ownership. In the United Kingdom, this view, when added to a commitment to the Welfare State and full employment, was termed "the postwar consensus."

Born: 1889, Vienna, Austria
Importance: Argued the case for limited government in the face of Keynesian orthodoxy
Died: 1992, Freiburg, Germany

F. A. Hayek, the champion of small government, did not accept the consensus view. As a classical liberal, he believed that the proper role of government was restricted to creating the conditions for individuals to pursue their own aims without hindrance. In his most famous work, *The Road to Serfdom*, he argued that the danger of central planning and government intervention was that it tended to lead to totalitarianism:

> Economic control is not merely control of a sector of human life which can be separated from the rest: it is the control of the means for all our ends.

Hayek's view, then, though it changed over time, was that the role of government should be restricted, more or less, to enforcing the rule of law. Thus, he rejected the idea, common in postwar Europe, that governments should manipulate the market in order to secure specific outcomes. In particular, he denied that the state should seek to promote material equality. Thus, for example, he argued against a progressive taxation system, where the rich pay a higher proportion of their earnings in tax than the poor, on the grounds that it violated the principle that individuals should be equal before the law.

Although, in some circles, Hayek's reputation is that of an uncaring zealot, like many intellectuals of his generation he was haunted by the specter of National Socialism and Stalinism. It was his view that minimal government was the best way to defend the kinds of freedoms that these totalitarian societies had sought to eradicate. He did not think that it was possible to plan centrally and also preserve individual liberty. Attempts to control the spontaneous functioning of a society would inevitably result in a move toward totalitarianism. Hayek also recognized that political commitments run deep and that convincing people on this point would be difficult.

> That democratic socialism...is not only unachievable, but that to strive for it produces something so utterly different that few of those who wish it would be prepared to accept the consequences, many will not believe until the connection has been laid bare in all its aspects.

For most of the second half of the twentieth century, Hayek's views were those of a minority. The postwar consensus, based on the economic theories of John Maynard Keynes, dominated politics and economics in the West until the 1980s. However, things began to shift. The governments of Margaret Thatcher, in the United Kingdom, and Ronald Reagan, in America, were advocates of small government. Hayek's reputation soared, and he is now considered the equal of Keynes, the twentieth century's other great economist.

Totalitarianism: A system of government which is based on the absolute power and authority of a single political actor (whether it be a person or a political party), where this power and authority penetrate deeply into the political, social, and cultural life of the society. Nazi Germany and Stalin's Soviet Union are paradigmatic examples of totalitarian societies.

Antonio Gramsci

There is a certain kind of deterministic Marxism which holds that the transition to communism is inevitable; that it will occur almost mechanistically as a result of the contradictions which exist in the economic base of capitalist society. Antonio Gramsci spent most of his intellectual life arguing against this kind of crude "economism"; indeed, he thought that this way of thinking was indicative of a certain naïveté, or "primitive infantilism," as he put it.

Born: 1891, Ales, Sardinia
Importance: Influential in Marxist circles, particularly for developing the concept of hegemony
Died: 1937, Rome, Italy

It was Gramsci's view that capitalism is much more resilient than many deterministic Marxists realized. This is because the proletariat (i.e., the working class), the class designated to bring down capitalism, is subject to the hegemonic control of the bourgeoisie (i.e., the ruling class). He meant by this that civil society is permeated by a whole edifice of beliefs, values, customs, and practices, which, in one way or another, shore up the established order and the class interests which dominate it. In other words, the proletariat remain subservient to the bourgeoisie because they have been incorporated within its ideological project.

Part of the importance of the idea of hegemony is that it explains why the proletariat have failed to develop the revolutionary consciousness that Marx predicted. The contradictions which lie at the heart of capitalism will not automatically lead to its collapse, because the bourgeoisie dominate the "superstructural" elements of society — for example, the media, the education system, and the legal system. This has important implications for the kinds of revolutionary strategy which are likely to be successful.

Gramsci distinguished between a "war of maneuver" and a "war of position." In situations where the bourgeoisie do not have hegemonic control — as, for example, in Russia in 1917 — a war of maneuver — that is, a quick revolutionary war — can work. However, this is not the case in modern Western societies, where "the superstructures of civil society are like the trench systems of modern warfare," enabling capitalism to survive its periodic crises.

In this situation, a war of position is required. This involves a struggle for the ideological hegemony of the proletariat. Roughly speaking, it is necessary for the proletariat and its allied classes to be incorporated within the project for revolutionary change. Until this is happens, the transition to socialism will not occur.

The importance of Gramsci's work is that it added a layer of sophistication to the standard Marxist conceptual framework. However, there is a slightly disturbing air of unfalsifiability about his ideas. If capitalism doesn't collapse, it isn't because there is no reason to expect it to, but rather because the proletariat have been blinded to their true destiny as an emancipatory force by bourgeois hegemony. In other words, Gramsci's default position is that capitalism is inherently unstable, and that revolution is only ever one war of position away. This has indeed been the standard Marxist line; revolution is just around the corner. The trouble is, at the beginning of the twenty-first century, it just isn't very plausible anymore.

Hegemony: In its most general sense, hegemony is the control and/or authority which one group exercises over another. The important point, however, is that control and authority can be achieved by means other than force. Thus, for example, a powerful group might make genuine concessions to a less powerful group in order to maintain its overall power.

John Dewey

The contemporary philosopher Richard Rorty has notoriously defined truth, presumably with his tongue at least somewhere near his cheek, as "whatever one's contemporaries let one get away with." Rorty is part of a tradition in philosophy which rejects the idea that "truth" is to be found in the correspondence between truth-claims and states of affair of the world. Perhaps the most important strand in this tradition is the pragmatism of philosophers such as Americans William James and John Dewey.

Born: 1859, Burlington, Vermont
Importance: A founder of the philosophical school of pragmatism
Died: 1952, New York

According to Dewey, the measure of any true belief is that it is useful; or, more precisely, that it provides successful rules for conduct in our dealings with the world. Normally, people get by in their everyday lives because they have access to a whole set of established and socially sanctioned habits. However, occasionally these habits break down; the actions and responses which people can draw upon prove inadequate in terms of the situations which they face, and they cannot go on — perhaps, for example, a scientist will be unable to reconcile established scientific thinking with some new data that has come in from an experiment. At this point, there occurs the kind of genuine doubt which necessitates inquiry.

It is Dewey's claim that having identified that there is a difficulty which needs addressing, inquiry proceeds by means of the isolation of the significant elements of the problematic situation. Once this is achieved, it is necessary to determine a number of hypotheses in order to solve the difficulty. This is a creative, imaginative process, and it involves going beyond what is given in the situation:

... it is more or less speculative, adventurous ... it involves a leap, a jump, the propriety of which cannot be absolutely warranted in advance, no matter what precautions be taken.

The final stages in this process of inquiry involve working through the implications of the various hypotheses which are being entertained, and then, crucially, testing them experimentally. Resolution occurs with the incorporation of new beliefs into the framework of habits that allows people to act in accordance with the events in their lives. Truth is that which works.

> Since education is not a means to living, but is identical with the operation of living a life which is fruitful ... the only ultimate value which can be set up is just the process of living itself.
>
> John Dewey *Democracy and Education*

To accomplish this kind of reasoning, individuals must be capable of flexible and sophisticated thought. There are clear implications here for the way people should be educated. Particularly, Dewey argued that education should not be overly didactic in form; the idea is not simply to impart information for students to passively absorb. Rather, proper education aims to foster imaginative responses to new information and situations, by engaging students in active, cooperative practices of learning.

By the time Dewey died in 1952, pragmatism was attracting less interest from professional philosophers. However, his place as a major figure in the philosophical firmament is assured, as is his influence on educational theory and liberal, progessive thought.

Jean Piaget

Jean Piaget was one of the twentieth century's most important psychologists. He is best known for his theory of intellectual development, which holds that human beings possess a genetically determined timetable which governs the emergence of particular cognitive abilities. It was Piaget's claim that the way that a five-year-old understands the world is qualitatively different from the way that a twelve-year-old understands the world, which in turn is different from the way that an adult understands the world.

Born: 1896, Neuchâtel, Switzerland
Importance: Developed hugely influential theory of cognitive development
Died: 1980, Geneva, Switzerland

Piaget identified four discrete stages of development. The "sensorimotor stage" lasts for the first two years of a child's life. The main achievement of this phase is the development of *object permanence*; that is, an awareness that the objects the child interacts with have a separate and independent existence. In the second stage, the "preoperational stage," which takes place roughly between the ages of two to seven, the child develops the ability to use and manipulate symbols and language. However, the facility to generalize beyond what is immediately given in experience has not yet emerged; the child lacks the ability to apply logical principles. The third, or "concrete operational stage," which runs from the age of seven to eleven, marks the beginnings of the child's ability to apply logical principles to objects. The child also becomes less egocentric in orientation, becoming aware that their viewpoint is only one among many. The final stage, the "formal operational stage," which normally starts between the ages of eleven and fifteen, is characterized by the ability to engage in decontextualized, abstract thought. It was Piaget's view that almost everybody

Left: Piaget thought that intellectual development occurs in a predictable way, driven largely by genetic factors. A five-year-old lives in a very different intellectual world than a newly born baby.

will attain this stage of development by the time that they are twenty years old.

According to Piaget, intellectual development, hardwired into every individual's genes, is driven by a process of "assimilation," "disequilibrium," and "accommodation." The idea here is that the child makes use of behavioral and mental schemas in order to make sense of the world. If the child confronts a genuinely new experience, then she will not be able to *assimilate* the experience to the existing schema. This results in a state of *disequilibrium*. The way out of this impasse is to change the existing schema in order to *accommodate* the new experience, thereby re-establishing a state of equilibrium. It is by this general process of adaptation that intellectual progress occurs.

Piaget's theories are not without their critics. For example, it has been claimed that it is not possible to identify the discrete stages of development which he postulated. However, his work has been tremendously influential, particularly in the field of education. Not least, it suggests that even if intellectual development occurs in a relatively predictable fashion, the child is best aided in this process by an active learning situation, which stresses experimentation and interaction with the environment.

Lawrence Kohlberg

Imagine that a woman is dying. There is one drug that might save her, but it is only available in a single shop, where it is on sale for $10,000. The woman's husband, Heinz, tries to borrow the money, but he only manages to get together about half the drug's cost. He goes to the shopkeeper, tells him that his wife is dying, and begs him to sell the drug for less, or to let him pay the balance at a later date. The shopkeeper says "No," despite the fact that he would still make a large profit on the sale. The husband is so desperate that in the end he breaks into the shop to steal the drug.

Born: 1927, Bronxville, New York
Importance: Outlined a highly original stage theory of moral development
Died: 1987, Boston

The psychologist Lawrence Kohlberg used scenarios like this, a version of his famous "Heinz dilemma," to work out a "stage theory" of moral development. He showed that at *different* stages of their intellectual development, people will give different reasons for the moral judgments that they make. Thus, for example, a young child will give different reasons for the conclusions that they draw about Heinz's behavior than the reasons given by an adult. What is important isn't whether a given action is judged right or wrong — whether it is thought that Heinz was right to steal the drug or not — but rather the reasoning process that leads them to the judgment.

Kohlberg identified three levels of moral development, each in turn comprising two stages. At the first, "pre-conventional," level, notions of right and wrong are determined by authority and the possibility of punishment; and then, at the second stage of the level, by whether or not an action will bring reward. Thus, for example, a young child might think that Heinz behaved badly because he is likely to get caught and punished. At the "conventional level," which is attained by most adolescents and adults, moral reasoning is tied closely to membership of wider social groups. At the first stage of this level, a good action is thought to be one which will gain the approval of others; at the second stage, one which is lawful and dutiful. The third, "post-conventional," level of moral development — in Kohlberg's view, only attained by about one-fifth of the population — is much more abstract in nature. Thus, moral reasoning at the second stage of this level, almost never achieved, involves reference to universal notions such as justice, human dignity, the sanctity of human life, and so on.

Kohlberg's importance is that he showed, with some sophistication, how moral development is linked to cognitive development. He did not think that moral development occurs *inevitably* as a result of growing older; it requires that individuals work on, think about, and discuss their processes of moral reasoning. Individuals cannot skip stages in their moral development, but rather have to come to appreciate the appropriateness of the stage of development immediately above their own. Therefore, in order to help people to advance to the highest levels, it is necessary, as John Dewey advised, to construct education systems in which people are actively involved in their own learning. Moral sophistication is something to be accomplished, not something to be handed down by authority.

Noam Chomsky

Prior to Noam Chomsky's book *Syntactic Structures*, published in 1957, the dominant theory of language development, as developed by thinkers such as B. F. Skinner, held that children acquire language as a result of training and experience (and, in particular, by the mechanism of selective reinforcement). Chomsky's view was quite different. He argued that human beings are born with an innate ability to understand the principles that underpin the structure of language. It is this which explains how language users are able to produce and comprehend an infinite range of sentences even though they will have only ever heard a tiny fraction of them before.

Born: 1928, Philadelphia
Importance: Argued that humans have an innate ability to understand the structure of language
Died:

It was Chomsky's claim that this ability rests on the fact that humans are able to move between two different levels of the structure of language. Consider, for example, these two phrases: "The cat ate the mouse" and "The mouse was eaten by the cat." They both have the same underlying meaning (deep structure), yet the two sentences look different, they have different surface structures. In simple terms, Chomsky's idea is that people are able to utter meaningful sentences because they have access to a set of "transformational rules" that allows them to convert the meaning of what they want to say (that the mouse ended up as the cat's dinner) into particular words and phrases ("The cat ate the mouse"). Thus, the meaning of a sentence is constituted by its deep structure, and our aptitude for language resides in our ability to transform deep structure into surface structure — that is, meaning into words and phrases — by means of a set of innate, universal, abstract rules.

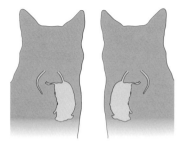

Left: The two phrases "The cat ate the mouse" and "The mouse was eaten by the cat" look different on the surface, yet they mean the same thing. Either way, the mouse ended up as the cat's dinner.

The evidence for something like Chomsky's view is quite persuasive. As we have already noted, the number of sentences which children are ever exposed to is but a tiny fraction of the number which they are able to generate. Also, the mechanism by which children are exposed to language, the spoken word, is an imperfect medium; people talk in incomplete sentences, they slur, make mistakes, and in other ways corrupt the surface structure of their utterances. Yet children still learn language. And they do so naturally, without much explicit guidance from the community of language users. According to Chomsky, these, and other factors, can only be accounted for by the existence of an innate Language Acquisition Device.

Chomsky's work on transformational-generative grammar, though never in its detail a majority view, revolutionized linguistics in the second half of the twentieth century. It is perhaps a shame, then, that he is now better known for his political views than as a linguist, for it is clear that people will be talking about his contribution to linguistics long after they have forgotten his politics.

> Colorless green ideas sleep furiously.
>
> Noam Chomsky
> *Syntactic Structures*

Mary Wollstonecraft

Mary Wollstonecraft was not so much a brilliant, original philosopher as a radical thinker in the mold of Thomas Paine. Like Paine, she thought that artificial distinctions of rank undermined the potential for human flourishing; and also that republicanism was preferable to hereditary monarchy as a form of government. However, she differed from Paine in one crucial respect; as well as advocating the rights of man, she advocated the rights of women.

Born: 1759, London, England
Significance: The first modern advocate of the rights of women
Died: 1797, London, England

Wollstonecraft subscribed to the Enlightenment view that society should be structured in such a way as to allow people to fulfil their potentials as rational beings. Unfortunately, the world in which she lived was a long way from meeting this ideal. In particular, women were being brought up in a way which stifled their intellectual and rational capabilities; they were taught to defer to men, and to cultivate a docile sexuality with which to attract and flatter them. It was Wollstonecraft's view that it wasn't only women who suffered as a result, but also men. If women were able to share the rights of men, then they would also mirror their virtues.

The major source of the inequality of women was their education. Thus, in the introduction to *A Vindication of the Rights of Women*, Wollstonecraft writes that she had looked at the "various books written on the subject of education, and patiently observed the conduct of parents and the management of schools...what has been the result? A profound conviction that the neglected education of my fellow-creatures is the grand source of the misery I deplore." In particular, women were taught that their character is the opposite of that of men; that it is in their nature to live entirely for others; and that to be sexually attractive they must be meek, submissive, and eager to please.

Wollstonecraft believed that the situation would only improve for women if there were changes in the way in which they were educated. In particular, unlike Rousseau, she argued that women should be educated in the same general way as men; that they should be encouraged to cultivate their rational capabilities. Thus, she argued that the "most perfect education ... is such an exercise of the understanding as is best calculated to strengthen the body and form the heart. Or, in other words, to enable the individual to attain such habits of virtue as will render it independent."

Wollstonecraft's message was undoubtedly radical for its time. However, it would be a mistake to think that she was advocating an entirely modern form of feminism. She thought, for example, that a woman's primary duty was to be a mother; albeit this should not involve her subjugation to a man. Nevertheless, she remains an inspiration to feminists; and although she was not the first person to advocate the rights of women, her importance is such that it is fair to consider her the first feminist.

> Women are systematically degraded by receiving the trivial attentions which men think it manly to pay to the sex, when, in fact, men are insultingly supporting their own superiority.
>
> Mary Wollstonecraft
> *A Vindication of the Rights of Woman*

J. S. Mill

John Stuart Mill is perhaps best known for his book *Utilitarianism*, in which, developing an idea originally conceived by Jeremy Bentham, he outlined his "Greatest Happiness Principle," which holds that "actions are right in proportion as they tend to promote happiness, wrong as they tend to produce the reverse of happiness." However, he also has a significant reputation as a logician, a radical liberal, and, perhaps most interestingly, as an early feminist.

Born: 1806, London, England
Importance: Argued the case for liberalism in an era of great reform
Died: 1873, Avignon, France

In *The Subjection of Women*, Mill set out to demonstrate that the subordination of women is "wrong in itself," and that "it ought to be replaced by a principle of perfect equality." He was aware that his arguments would meet strong resistance; the majority of men had opinions about women's rightful station that were rooted in feelings that were unlikely to be altered by rational argument. Nevertheless, he aimed to show how the prejudices of his age gained their power from the malign rather than admirable aspects of human nature.

He argued that the subordination of women was a curious phenomenon in modern societies, since these tend to be meritocratic. In the modern world, people are not normally compelled by dint of their births to live out particular kinds of lives, as would have been the case, for example, for a person born to a slave in Ancient Greece. Modern societies are governed according to the principle that individuals are "free to employ their faculties, and such favorable chances as offer, to achieve the lot which may appear to them most desirable." According to Mill, if this is true, then it should also apply to women; the fact that a person is born a girl, rather than a boy, should not determine the course of her life. That it does, "stands out as an isolated fact of modern social institutions; a solitary breach of what has become their fundamental law; a single relic of an old world of thought and practice ..."

Mill rejected the idea that there were essential differences between men and women which might justify women's subordination. He held that it wasn't possible to tell what mental and moral differences there were between the sexes, since the nature of women had been so thoroughly distorted by their subordination. Moreover, even if it turned out that men and women were different, this would not be grounds for denying them equality of opportunity; thus, for example, the fact that women on average might be physically slightly weaker than men is no good reason for excluding those women who are strong enough for certain kinds of physical work from doing that work.

> The principle which regulates the existing social relations between the two sexes — the legal subordination of one sex to the other — is wrong in itself, and now one of the chief hindrances to human improvement.
>
> J. S. Mill *The Subjection of Women*

Mill's arguments in *The Subjection of Women*, unlike those of some of the other early feminists, stand the test of time. This is perhaps not surprising, for he is generally considered to be one of the nineteenth century's great intellects.

Simone de Beauvoir

Simone de Beauvoir, although a major philosopher in her own right, is perhaps best known for her relationship with Jean-Paul Sartre. This fact, as well as unfair, is deeply ironical, for Beauvoir is probably the twentieth century's most important feminist thinker. Moreover, the main argument of perhaps her most significant book, *The Second Sex*, is precisely that women tend to be defined as "the Other" of men.

Born: 1908, Paris, France
Importance: Her book *The Second Sex* sparked a new wave of feminism, and remains a key feminist text
Died: 1986, Paris, France

Although the idea of the Other might sound commonsensical, it actually involves quite a bit of complicated existential analysis. The notion can be traced back to Hegel's dialectic of the Master and Slave. Simply, it was Hegel's claim that people define themselves as autonomous subjects by dominating their fellows (the Other). Beauvoir took this idea, which had been developed by Sartre, and applied it to the relationship between men and women. Thus, in the introduction to *The Second Sex*, she argued that woman "is defined and differentiated with reference to man and not he with reference to her; she is the incidental, the inessential, as opposed to the essential. He is the Subject, he is the Absolute — she is the Other."

> It is not in giving life but in risking life that man is raised above the animal; that is why superiority has been accorded in humanity not to the sex that brings forth but to that which kills.
>
> Simone de Beauvoir
> *Second Sex*

Beauvoir also makes use of two further Hegelian terms, transcendence and immanence, in order to analyze the relationship between the sexes. Men manifest their transcendence in freely embarking on projects, primarily in the work sphere, which define their relationship to the world. Women, on the other hand, are condemned to immanence; to the repetition of the mundane tasks of everyday existence, particularly, those involved in their roles as mothers, housekeepers, and the objects of male sexual desire. Beauvoir does not believe that men have actually taken away the freedom of women; this would run counter to her existentialism which holds that every person is necessarily free. Rather, women are perceived, and perceive themselves to be, naturally inferior to men; their status as the Other seems a natural function of womanhood. In other words, inferiority is embedded in the idea of "the eternal feminine." Part of what it is to be a woman is to be man's Other.

To the extent that female inferiority appears natural, women are frequently complicit in their own oppression. It is a common theme in existentialism that there are certain advantages in the denial of freedom. Beauvoir develops this idea and argues, for example, that women, rather than pursuing their own free projects, might prefer the security of lives defined in terms of their attachment to particular men.

Needless to say, it is Beauvoir's view that the idea of the "eternal feminine" is illusory. As the most famous line in *The Second Sex* has it, "One is not born, but rather becomes, a woman." In order to achieve freedom, then, women must reject those conceptions of womanhood which confine them to lives of dull repetition and drudgery.

Existentialism: A philosophical approach that emphasizes the primacy of individual existence, rejecting the idea that humans have fundamental essences which are somehow separate from their particular lives. It is also frequently associated with, variously, the idea that humans are necessarily free, moral skepticism (i.e., the denial that there are objective, binding moral codes), atheism, and a concern with the possibility of living authentically.

Kate Millett

Kate Millett's groundbreaking work, *Sexual Politics*, which outlined a theory of patriarchy, was a central text of the second wave of feminism in the early 1970s. She claimed that the relationship between the sexes is characterized by female subordination. Indeed, it was her argument that patriarchal government, the institution whereby females are controlled by males, is characteristic, in varying degrees, of all historical societies.

Born: 1934, St. Paul, Minnesota
Importance: By developing the concept of patriarchy, played a major role in the second wave of feminism
Died:

Millett denied that biological factors were the cause of the pervasiveness of patriarchy. Indeed, beyond the obvious physical differences between the sexes, there was, she argued, no convincing evidence that the sexes were biologically different in an important way. In her view, it was clear that gender — the temperament and behavior associated with the two sexes — was overwhelmingly a social construct; that is, that it was culturally produced. This applies even to sexuality, which "is almost entirely the product of learning. So much is this the case that even the act of coitus itself is the product of a long series of learned responses — responses to the patterns and attitudes, even as to the object of sexual choice, which are set up for us by our social environment."

According to Millett, patriarchy gains its legitimacy through the functioning of socialization. Thus, for example, human personalities are formed in terms of prescribed, stereotypical sex identities. Women learn to be passive, docile, and ineffectual; whereas men are taught to be aggressive, intelligent, and effective. This difference in temperament is complemented and reinforced by the different roles which are attached to each gender. Women are confined primarily to a domestic role; indeed, Millett goes so far as to argue that the role of women does little to separate them from animals; they give birth and they look after children. In contrast, men pursue activities which are "distinctly human"; their interests and ambitions extend well beyond domestic service and the care of infants.

The ideas outlined in *Sexual Politics* provoked strong criticism. Conservative critics, after she disclosed her own bisexuality, dismissed Millett as a man-hating lesbian. Feminist critics, for their part, claimed that the idea that patriarchy had effectively infantilized women was to denigrate women, and to overestimate the extent of male power. She was also criticized for overstating the role of culture in the construction of sexual and gender identities. Nevertheless, her work remains hugely important. Andrea Dworkin, another leading light of the second wave of feminism, has said that she "cannot think of anyone who accomplished what Kate Millett did, with this one book. It remains the alpha and omega of the women's movement. Everything that feminists have done is foreshadowed, predicted, or encouraged by *Sexual Politics*."

> However muted its present appearance may be, sexual domination obtains nevertheless as perhaps the most pervasive ideology of our culture and provides its most fundamental concept of power.
>
> Kate Millett *Sexual Politics*

Feminism

Philosophy has not always treated women well. Aristotle, for example, said that the reason that women did not grow bald was because their nature was very similar to that of children; and G. F. Hegel opined that men "correspond to animals, while women correspond to plants because their development is more placid and the principle that underlies it is the rather vague unity of feeling." These attitudes, of course, are a reflection of the fact that women have been in various ways subordinate to men in probably every human society that has ever existed.

Feminists, while agreeing that this is a bad thing, are at odds with each other about how it has happened. Radical feminists link the subordination of women to patriarchy — the political, social, and cultural dominance of men over women — a characteristic of all historical societies. There is no general agreement about how patriarchy got started, but most radical feminists agree that it is maintained by the cultural reproduction of exploitative gender roles; in other words, in the service of men, women are taught how to be "women."

Some feminists are worried by what they see as the inflexibility of the concept of patriarchy. They point out that there are radical differences in the statuses enjoyed by particular women; that badly off women often have more in common with badly-off men than they do with well-off women; and that there are other groups in society that are also oppressed and exploited, particularly certain social classes and ethnic groups. Friedrich Engels suggested that the subordination of women is linked to the exploitative nature of capitalist society: women are oppressed because they are confined within the domestic sphere in order to ensure clear lines of descent so that men can pass on property to their natural heirs. Abolish class-based society, and you abolish the oppression of women.

However, the idea that it is possible to create a society without sexual differences is highly contentious. It could be that sexual inequality is linked to differences in biology. Helena Cronin, for example, has argued that because natural selection has favored males with an appetite for multiple mates, they have a greater tendency than women to be "competitive, risk-taking, opportunistic, persevering, single-minded, inclined to display, to show off. That is why men are more likely to die heroically, win a Nobel prize, drive too fast, commit murder."

If Cronin is right, then sexual equality, while no doubt an admirable goal, might be hard to achieve. Certainly, despite huge progress over the last fifty years or so, there is still a long way to go. Women almost everywhere are the primary caregivers; they are overwhelmingly the targets of domestic abuse; and in countries around the world, they are oppressed in the name of religion. Feminism's task, then, has only just begun.

> For him she is sex — absolute sex, no less. She is defined and differentiated with reference to man and not he with reference to her; she is the incidental, the inessential as opposed to the essential. He is the Subject, he is the Absolute — she is the Other.
>
> Simone de Beauvoir
> *Second Sex*

George Santayana

George Santayana was not only a philosopher of repute; he was also highly regarded as a poet, novelist, and literary critic. It is not surprising then that, in the early part of his philosophical career especially, he was interested in aesthetics; that is, in the study and nature of beauty.

Born: 1863, Madrid, Spain
Importance: Developed a naturalistic approach to esthetics
Died: 1952, Rome, Italy

His philosophical approach was naturalistic in character; he thought that philosophy should start in "the middle of things," in the lived world, rather than in the realm of abstract, rational contemplation. This applied as much to his ideas about aesthetics, as it did to his more general philosophical work on epistemology and ontology. He outlined his theory of aesthetics in *The Sense of Beauty*, his first major work. The task he set himself was to discuss "why, when, and how beauty appears, what conditions an object must fulfil to be beautiful, what elements of our nature make us sensible of beauty, and what the relation is between the constitution of the object and the excitement of our susceptibility."

> On the whole the world has seemed to me to move in the direction of light and reason, not that reason can ever govern human affairs, but that illusions and besetting passions may recede from the minds of men and allow reason to shine there.
>
> George Santayana *Letters*

He determined that beauty is the pleasure of contemplating an object, where that pleasure is conceived as being a character of the object itself. Beauty is a "value"; it is not the perception of some fact about the world, since to approach the world scientifically is not to approach it aesthetically, but rather "it is an emotion, an affection of our volitional and appreciative nature." In contrast to morality, which also has to do with what we value, beauty does not have a negative aspect; its value is "positive, intrinsic, and objectified."

Perhaps the most puzzling part of Santayana's conception is the idea that pleasure might come to be seen as an intrinsic part of an object. This seems paradoxical; pleasure is subjective, objects aren't. However, on further reflection, it isn't such a strange idea. Consider, for example, the experience of standing on the top of a hill on a beautifully sunny day, gazing at the vista below. It is easy to see how one's pleasure in such a moment might "infect" the objects of one's contemplation, so that it is taken to be an aspect of those objects. Beauty then "is an emotional element, a pleasure of ours, which nevertheless we regard as a quality of things."

There is no general agreement among critics about the importance of the ideas which Santayana outlined in *The Sense of Beauty*. It is felt by some that by locating beauty in the *experience* of pleasure, he pays insufficient regard to the form or the content of the objects which elicit pleasure. However, he is praised by others for bringing "beauty down to earth"; and in the preface to the 1955 edition of the work he is credited with bringing American aesthetics to maturity.

Ontology: The study of being or existence. Thus, for example, to claim that the universe is made of physical stuff — stuff that has extension and a spatio-temporal location — is to make an ontological claim (because it is a claim about the nature of reality).

Herbert Marcuse

To be a Marxist living in the West in the period immediately after World War II was in many ways not easy. Capitalism, far from crumbling, seemed uncommonly healthy. It was a time of near full employment, rapid technological advancement, and growing consumerism. Revolution, communist or otherwise, seemed a million miles away. Marxism, if it were to remain credible, needed a fresh impetus, a new direction which would maintain its relevance in the latter part of the century.

Born: 1898, Berlin, Germany
Importance: Combined Marxism and psychoanalysis to create a radical critique of capitalist society
Died: 1979, Starnberg, Germany

With his book *Eros and Civilization*, Herbert Marcuse aimed to provide this by knitting together Marxism and Freudianism in order to develop a radical critique of capitalist society. A central plank of Freudian theory has it that the libidinal energies of human beings are subject to a reality principle, whereby they are repressed in the interests of self-preservation (thus, for example, it isn't possible for humans to spend their whole time having sex because they must also feed and clothe themselves). Marcuse developed this idea to argue that the level of repression varies according to the demands of particular societies. In capitalism, which is based on class exploitation, there exists a "performance principle" which demands surplus-repression; that is, in the interests of the ruling class, the repression of libidinal energies goes beyond what is required for self-preservation.

According to Marcuse, there were good reasons to believe that this situation might come to an end. Capitalism, by virtue of the technological advances brought about by its performance principle, had, in effect, abolished economic scarcity. This meant that there was no longer any need for surplus-repression, which in turn held out the prospect of radical social change. It was Marcuse's belief that if surplus-repression were eradicated, then the consequent release of libidinal energies would result in a qualitatively different individual and social existence.

However, while the message of *Eros and Civilization* was essentially optimistic, by the time he came to write *One-Dimensional Man* in the mid-1960s he had become much more pessimistic about the possibilities for radical social change. In this work, he argued that the super-abundance of capitalist societies had rendered the working class impotent, through the production of an

> The people recognize themselves in their commodities; they find their soul in their automobile, hi-fi set, split-level home, kitchen equipment.
>
> Herbert Marcuse
> *One-Dimensional Man*

edifice of "false needs" — through the effects of advertising, for example — which in effect dominates individuals by depriving them of real choices. In this situation, a critical Marxism remains necessarily abstract; the social movements by which social change might be effected simply do not exist.

Although the upheavals of the late 1960s led to Marcuse rediscovering some of his optimism, it is reasonable to conclude, with hindsight, that the pessimism of *One-Dimensional Man* was justified. Communist revolution, especially after the collapse of the Soviet Union, seems further away than ever. However, this point necessarily affects any assessment of Marcuse's significance as a philosopher. Marxism seems now almost a historical oddity; the importance of Marcuse's ideas is diminished as a result.

Jacques Derrida

The work of Jacques Derrida, the originator of deconstructionism, is notoriously difficult to understand. Partly this is because he employs a deliberately experimental and provocative writing style. For example, in the work *Glas*, he divides each page into two columns; one column deals with Hegel, the other with the writer Genet, but, at the same time, the two columns subtly engage with each other. He also has a fondness for neologism — the coining of new words — and literary effect.

Born: 1930, El Biar, Algeria
Importance: The originator of deconstruction, a method of textual analysis
Died: 2004, Paris, France

Consider, for instance, the definition of the word "sign," which appears in *Of Grammatology*, perhaps his most famous work:

> … the sign ~~is~~ that ill-named ~~thing~~, the only one, that escapes the instituting question of philosophy: "what is …?"

As in the work of the German philosopher Martin Heidegger, the crossings-out place words "under erasure." The idea is to indicate that the erased words — which it is necessary to use, because there are no better alternatives — in some way miss or exceed their intended meaning.

The notion that meaning is slippery, complex, multifaceted, and indeterminate is perhaps the central theme of Derrida's work. Thus, deconstruction, simply put, refers to a way of reading texts that throws their meaning radically in doubt. Normally when reading a text, we treat words as if they have a determinate meaning linked to the way that they refer to things in the world. Deconstructionism rejects this way of approaching a text, arguing that it is based on an unwarranted "metaphysics of presence."

Derrida

Instead, a deconstructionist reading of a text might aim to determine what it doesn't say; the idea being that what is absent in a text might tell you a lot about what is present. Or one might look for hidden contradictions or ambiguities in a text; for the way in which a text undermines itself. Deconstruction, then, is fundamentally about penetrating beneath the surface appearance of things in order to bring out hidden layers of articulation.

All this might seem unobjectionable. After all, people have been analyzing texts for hidden meaning for centuries. However, there is a problem here in that Derrida sometimes seems to suggest that the indeterminate nature of language, and the self-referential nature of texts, mean that words never refer to states of affair in the world, and that, therefore, the distinction between truth and fiction is rendered moot. Thus, for example, in *Of Grammatology*, Derrida claimed that there "is nothing outside the text"; and, elsewhere, he argued that the "absence of the transcendental signified extends the domain and the play of signification infinitely."

This kind of thing has made philosophers trained in the more restrained Anglophone tradition very suspicious. Thus, Derrida's reputation as a philosopher is characterized by schism: to some, he is one of the twentieth century's most important thinkers; to others, he is a charlatan, who used linguistic complexity to disguise a paucity of real thought.

Postmodernism

Postmodernism is a term which is bandied around with merry abandon despite the fact that it doesn't really have a clear meaning. Indeed, it is notoriously difficult to give any definition of postmodernism, or to distill its essence for the purposes of summary. Perhaps, then, the best starting place to get a sense of what it involves is to take one particular area, say movies, and to consider what it is that makes a movie "postmodern."

Postmodern movies are extremely common, even in mainstream filmmaking, such as the three *Scream* movies, the *Scream* parody, *Scary Movie* (which also, incidentally, parodies postmodernism), and *The Brady Bunch Movie*. These films share a number of things which mark them out as postmodern. They are all, in various ways, self-referential. Thus, for example, the characters in *Scream* discuss what would likely happen to them if they were in a horror movie; and in *Scary Movie*, the self-referential aspect of the postmodern horror genre is itself exaggerated for comic effect; the movie begins, for example, with an absurd parody of a scene from the *Exorcist*, which functions to parody parody.

In their self-referential aspects, these movies also indicate that what we see does not refer to or represent anything in the "real" world. So unlike a movie such as *The Blair Witch Project*, which was filmed in a particular way specifically to suggest authenticity, the *Scream* movies leave the audience in no doubt that they are watching a fictional construct. Indeed, more than this, the *Scream* films exhibit a kind of "knowingness," which suggests not only that they are fictional constructs, but that all movies are the same, whatever their artistic intent.

These attributes of ironic self-reference, and a denial that there is anything beyond mere appearance — that there is no real world to be represented — are characteristics of postmodernism in general. Thus, for example, in philosophy, postmodern approaches deny the possibility that texts — or, indeed, language — can represent the real world. Jacques Derrida, for instance, has criticized what he calls "the metaphysics of presence," the idea that determinate meaning resides in words themselves which refer to things in the real world.

In movies, postmodernism is fun. In philosophy, its effect has been much more sinister. Its adherents have often taken its insights to mean that it is not possible to tell the truth about the world. This has potentially devastating philosophical and political consequences. If, for example, there is no truth about whether the Holocaust took place, how is it possible to counter holocaust denial? These kinds of thoughts have led large numbers of people to turn away from postmodernist ideas, so much so that talk of post-postmodernism is now common.

> The postmodern would be that which, in the modern, puts forward the unpresentable in presentation itself; that which denies itself the solace of good forms, the consensus of a taste which would make it possible to share collectively the nostalgia for the unattainable; that which searches for new presentations ... in order to impart a stronger sense of the unpresentable.
>
> Jean Francois-Lyotard
> *What Is Postmodernism?*

Index

For main philosopher entries see contents pages. References to philosophers are given only where mentioned other than their main entry.